PIONEER PADDLES of the COLONIAL SOUTH

by WILLIAM D. AUMAN

For all who share in the spirit of the Paddle

MANGROVE MOUNTAIN
PRESS

Pioneer Paddles of the Colonial South

Copyright © 2026 William D. Auman

Print ISBN: 979-8-9944264-0-1
Ebook ISBN: 979-8-9944264-1-8

Library of Congress Control Number 2026901543
Auman, William D., Pioneer Paddles of the Colonial South

All rights reserved. No part of this publication may be reproduced, stored in a retrieval system, or transmitted in any form or by any means, electronic, mechanical, photocopying, recording, or otherwise, without the written permission of the author.

This book is printed on acid-free paper.

Front/Back Cover photos: The author's 1988 Great Canadian Huron cedar strip canoe, built by First Nations tribal member Maurice Pritchard.

Printed in the United States of America.
First Edition 2026 – Mangrove Mountain Press
New Port Richey, Florida

William D. Auman

PROLOGUE

Listen closely as the wind rushes past your canoe or kayak, with gentle waves and salt spray rippling across the western horizon of the Gulf of Mexico, ancient home of the Calusa. The drum beat is faint, but the spirits live on. In times of quiet, all is calm. Close your eyes and the chorus of those from a bygone era begins to echo in rhythm with the stroke of your paddle. For a moment you may enter the surreal and envision the aura of the pirate or privateer, perhaps the legendary Henry Morgan or the mythical Jose Gaspar, seeking to pillage and plunder a majestic Spanish galleon, whose masts cast a shadow on the cypress dugouts of Indigenous Peoples, who saw their way of life change immensely over time...assuming they survived. Their nimble boats, filled with clam and oyster shells, quickly retreat into a maze of mangroves within the tidal bays of the Gulf. It may no longer be quiet and calm, but you awaken from the dream and all that remains is the thought of the déjà vu which was just experienced.

Such is the life of the paddler—an intricate connection to nature through solitude, observation, imagination, and appreciation for the historical wilderness that continues to harbor intrigue with secrets to unveil. We just have to open our minds, listen, learn, and continue the journey. The renowned inspirational author, Jack Kerouac, once said that "there was nowhere to go but everywhere, so just keep on rolling under the stars." That mantra can equally be applied to pioneer paddling, fostering an ambiance that obsessively nurtures the soul.

Pioneer Paddles of the Colonial South

Our paddling journeys over the past forty years or so have been consistently indexed into an ongoing database featuring over 400 different bodies of water. From Maine to Montana to Alaska, Algonquian Provincial Park to the Caribbean, the tales are too numerous to tell. However, after the initial publication of *Pioneer Paddling Colonial Carolina (2010)*, many readers have encouraged me to expand my colonial chronicles to include selected remaining areas of the southeast that are found within the region we know as home. The project was put on hold for many reasons, including the release of my first novel, *If Trees Could Testify...(2021)*, but turning a page in my career has finally allowed for the time to bring this project to fruition, pun intended.

Included within this work, in addition to an update of paddles within our native Old North State, are a number of historically-based journeys that paddlers with inquiring minds can enjoy, together with an intertwined dose of stories that may resonate with those of a creative mindset. My data base has been narrowed due to certain parameters to chronicle 169 bodies of water in North Carolina, 86 in Florida, 41 in South Carolina, 19 in Tennessee, 18 in Georgia and 12 in Virginia. A primary purpose is to place emphasis upon that which offers the highest degree of options for the reader from a base of our own personal experiences within the southeastern geographic region, so that they can best create their own adventures. Although focus is centered within favorited areas of Florida and North Carolina, a variety of excursions are also featured from coastal Georgia, South Carolina and Virginia, with added segments of eastern Tennessee that were known to legendary frontiersmen such as Daniel Boone and Davy Crockett.

William D. Auman

  The colonial-era south offers a myriad of possibilities for voyage and historical discovery, and it would take several human lifetimes to attempt to catalog each one. The temperate climate allows for year-round exploration of exponential paddling destinations, with no need to put that canoe or kayak into a winter dry dock. Consequently, as opposed to a comprehensive guide book, this effort is designed to cater to the "family-oriented" wilderness paddler from a personal perspective. In keeping with a familial theme, this book will emphasize non-technical trips that can appeal to even the most novice of paddlers. Special attention is given to locales that offer day trip options which may better accommodate families or those of us in perpetual "middle age" and who have evolved from the extremes of our younger selves.

  As my wife and I discovered long ago, the inquiring minds of young children serve to enhance the moments and engage the lifeline of history as a part of the surrounding environment. Our son and daughter received their canoeing baptisms at ages 3 and 2 respectively, and they continue to offer inspiration and insight when we are fortunate enough to have them along, as do our granddaughters. It is a heart-warming experience to watch young children (and/or one of our canine companions) splashing around in a body of water that is no more deep than they are tall, while the river rocks and rolls down its gentle slope around them. The sound of the stream is both persistent and soothing, with accompanying laughter creating a musical harmony all its own. In addition, there are always dinosaurs to seek out and turtles or birds to count along the way.

  On a personal level, I have been paddling since my

Pioneer Paddles of the Colonial South

parents gifted me my first boat back in 1973 at age 12. That opened the door to a passion that has remained throughout my life. I have worn many hats in my career, including a stint as a tennis professional, basketball coach, attorney and college professor, but have now morphed into what some consider to be a "hillbilly beachbum." That persona, applied through the lens of pioneer paddling, has evolved into a most consistent fit that sits best with my soul. My ideal journey is to embrace a creative mindset that leaves the world behind, paddle for an hour or so into a simpler time, locate a landing area that offers a nice respite to enjoy a cold beverage and a swim, then continue or return to the destination at hand. You will find that many of those such moments can be had while exploring the pioneer paddles recounted herein.

Our human composition was definitely designed for a life prior to the takeover of technologically-based contemporary civilization, before sirens and the sounds of engines detracted from the pleasant sensation of an awakening breeze rushing through the branches of a surrounding forest. We all respond with positive excitement to the natural wonders of wilderness, a playground much more meaningful than what one can find staring at a smartphone, tablet or television screen. It is my goal to offer these experiences as a link to that from which we came, and foster a renewal of the spirit of discovery and connection which lies within all of us.

Enough of the monologue and on to the message. Let's hit the water and paddle through a mystical portal into history. Only a few strokes can take you and yours back to a simpler time.

William D. Auman

CHAPTER ONE

LA FLORIDA: from the Timucua to the Calusa

Section One: A Fountain of Youth may lead to Mermaids in the Northern Peninsula

The moment has come to engage the time-travel button on my kayak and venture back to an era before Native Americans discovered the lost European explorers, with *La Florida ("land of flowers")* an appropriate place to begin. We have paddled here since the early 1980s and are now fortunate to spend several months each winter exploring the state, which harbors an amazing variety of paddling options and wildlife viewing opportunities.

Long before the arrival of Ponce de Leon in 1513 and Pedro Menendez de Aviles in 1565, the Timucau people were fishing, hunting, and cultivating beans and squash in the region now known as St. Augustine in the northeastern corner of the state. The principal chief of the Timucau at the time Menendez arrived was known as Seloy, whose village has been located on the grounds of what is known today as the Fountain of Youth Park, about one mile north of the *Castillo de San Marcos*. Whereas I tend to prefer Cigar City's Tocobaga IPA, I have drunk from the pristine waters of the Fountain on several occasions and remember sitting in a cypress dugout canoe on display in the park as a child back in the 1960s. Although I don't always recognize the face that stares back at me in the mirror, I have been asked many times what I plan to do when I eventually grow up. Perhaps there is some truth to the mystique associated within the properties of the fountain after all?

Spanish for "St Mark's Castle," the Castillo is the oldest masonry fort in the continental United States and a sight to behold, particularly from the water when approaching from Matanzas Bay where it casts its sentinel shadow. Construction had been ordered in 1672 by Governor Francisco de la Guerra de la Vega after a raid by English privateer Robert Searle in 1668 had destroyed much of St. Augustine and damaged the existing wooden fort. Searle had also succeeded in freeing surgeon Henry Woodard, the first European settler of South Carolina, who had been captured by the Spanish and held at the fort. This occurred during a time when Florida was still a part of the Spanish Empire, but let's not get ahead of ourselves and thus return to the prior century for somewhat more context.

Although the Spanish were initially welcomed by the Timucua, history reveals that they did not return the hospitality, using their hosts to forcibly supply food, pottery and wives. In less than a year, the Timucua had had enough and the Spanish were driven across the bay to Anastasia Island where they established a town that was inhabited for six years, yet no trace of it has yet to be found. Before their evacuation, however, Menendez and crew had successfully attacked the French colonial settlement known as Fort Caroline, thought to be on the banks of the St. Johns River further inland near present-day Jacksonville.

William D. Auman

The adventurous paddler could choose to traverse the salt marsh that frames the Matanzas River and retrace the footprint of the cypress dugout canoes of the Timucua near their ancient village, potentially using the Vilano boat ramp for access. Chances are you would encounter a pod of Atlantic Bottlenose Dolphin as you ferry across the channel. Another option would be to access Salt Run from the Lighthouse Park boat ramp and cross the bay to hunt for evidence of the relocated Spanish town. Keep in mind, however, that both of these alternatives would likely entail maneuvering through significant 21st century motor boat traffic and choppy waves from their wake, so a true wilderness experience would be tempered. Accordingly, it would be my suggestion to embark slightly further south for one of the best colonial paddles that the First Coast has to offer, that being Fort Matanzas National Monument.

The European history of Fort Matanzas predates its construction by almost 200 years, for in 1565, roughly two weeks after Menendez's attack on Fort Caroline, 134 surviving French soldiers and settlers under the command of Jean Ribault were massacred on the north shore of the inlet. From that point on, the inlet was known as "Matanzas"—meaning "slaughter" in Spanish. The well-preserved Coquina Fort was subsequently

Fort Mantanzas viewed from the author's kayak

built by the Spanish in 1742 to guard the southern mouth of the river, which could easily serve as a back entrance to St. Augustine by invading parties. The Spanish used convicts, slaves and troops from Cuba to erect the structure, which ironically only saw battle as it was nearing completion in 1742 when its cannon fire repelled British ships under the command of James Edward Oglethorpe.

William D. Auman

A paddler can easily slide into the inlet off of A1A and enjoy a short day trip among the approximate 300 acres of dunes, marsh and maritime forests that remain protected to this day and contribute to the essence of days gone by. Alternatively, access is available at Schmidt Park on Rattlesnake Island just off of A1A. Legend has it that the ghosts of those summarily executed without due process of law still haunt these waters and their cries can be heard through the quiet breeze of a misty morning, or on the night of a full moon. Do listen carefully and take a moment to reflect, for the lessons of history can be doomed to repeat themselves when their meaning is forgotten.

One of those lessons from our complex social history is to be found at Fort Mose, the first legally sanctioned free Black settlement in what is now the southern United States, which is located just north of St. Augustine off of US 1. Established in 1738 by Spanish governor Manuel Montiano, any fugitive slaves discovered by the Spanish were directed to this sanctuary of sorts, where they would be treated as being free if they accepted Catholicism, were baptized with Christian names, and if deemed fit to do so, serve four years in the colonial militia. This was in the aftermath of King Charles II's 1693 royal decree proclaiming that runaway slaves could be granted asylum in Florida.

The fort was destroyed by Oglethorpe's army in 1740, just prior to his ill-fated attempt to attack Fort Matanzas, but was rebuilt by the Spanish in 1752 only to be destroyed again in 1812. One can still paddle the waterfront site of about 40 acres which lies off of Robinson's Creek along Florida's intercoastal waterway thanks to the use of a floating boardwalk platform just to the east of the museum, but be aware of the tide since higher water levels are required. Much of the undeveloped surrounding area probably looks comparable to how it did when Ponce de Leon first encountered it.

Numerous other "pioneer" paddling access points abound in the northern peninsula, with a few favorites specifically deserving mention. Let's remember that thousands of years before European conquest, the entire state was home to diverse cultures of Native Americans who were impacted by colonization in different ways with differing results. The dispossession of land was often ripe with war, deceit and distress. Arguably, the most well-known of the Florida tribes were the Seminoles, who were actually a collected group of refugees from various other tribes including the Creek *(aka Muskogee)*, Yemassee, and even some Cherokee, who fought for their sovereignty until the conclusion of the Third Seminole War in 1858. In the two decades prior, the remaining members of the Seminoles had been pushed south to the Everglades where their reservation, along with that of the Miccosukee *(originally a part of the Creek nation)*, can be found today. These determined people, pushed into hiding in places where they never would have lived by choice, but where troops bent on genocide could not follow, became a proud people that no army could conquer.

Returning to the water, a replica Creek Village from the 1700s can be found along the South Withlacoochee River near Dade City, and an amazing pre-Columbian six-mound complex can be paddled by on the Crystal River just north of the Homosassa River, where West Indian manatees (aka "sea cows") abound in the cooler months. This is an area known as Florida's Nature Coast, which extends from Wakulla County south into

Pasco County just north of Tarpon Springs. The Crystal River Archaeological Park was occupied for roughly 1,600 years, and includes burial mounds, temple mounds, a plaza area and a substantial shell midden.

Just south of the Homosassa lies the pristine spring-fed Chassahowitzka ("the Chaz"), and slightly further south we find the Weeki Wachee River and its mermaids, who are said to swim

Temple Mound along the Crystal River

alongside their faithful companion manatees in the river that always features a temperature in the low 70s. Keep a keen eye out for both mermaids and manatees alike whether you put in at Rogers Park for an upstream paddle or the state park which lies several miles further upstream so as to float down with the mild current. The sea cows can often be found and observed at "hospital hole" which is only about a mile above Rogers Park. If you opt for the Chaz, there is a convenient river campground to launch from and the nice folk who run it will give you a map to

Pioneer Paddles of the Colonial South

the springs where you can swim year round.

Virtually around the corner from Weeki Wachee you will find Bayport Park, the site of an archaic Native American encampment and from which you can launch to paddle the mangroves in the Gulf of Mexico that surround a tranquil lagoon. On July 3, 1864, the Union Army landed and left behind the remains of a Confederate ship which can be seen underneath the pier. The Jenkins Creek canoe trail is another option just down the road, as is the Pedersen Wilderness Preserve trail which lies across Florida Hwy 597 from the Jenkins access. Slightly south is the quaint village of Aripeka where the famous Yankee slugger known as Babe Ruth would often retreat to fish. Named for an early nineteenth-century Seminole chief who was thought to have lived nearby, the area features a short paddle loop beginning at Norfleet's Fish Camp for only a $5 launch fee. Abundant wading birds such as the anhinga, cormorant, egret and a variety of herons will accompany you on each of these paddles and osprey will dive bomb your boat from above if you venture too close to their nest.

Further inland, the crystalline Ichetucknee River flows six miles through shaded hammocks and wetlands before it joins the Santa Fe River, another worthy adventure. A 17th century Spanish mission site has been identified in the Ichetucknee Springs Park which served the Timucua chiefdom and a Seminole settlement subsequently inhabited the area as documented by U.S. Indian Agent Benjamin Hawkins in 1799. For a lakeshore out and back paddle, Lochloosa Lake in Alachua County has great bass fishing and associated legends from Burnt Island in its southeastern corner, made famous by notable author

William D. Auman

Marjorie Kinnan Rawlings.

Other recommended alternative treks in the northern region include the Rainbow River near Dunnellon and the majestic Suwannee, immortalized by composer Stephen Foster who wrote "Old Folks at Home" to honor the river. Varying access points offering paddles of different lengths for all of the above can best be found using a version of today's sextant known as an internet search, although each body of water can generally be paddled on an out-and-back basis. The Suwannee in particular has a myriad of options throughout its 246 mile waterway from the Okefenokee Swamp to the Gulf of Mexico. Aspiring adventurers should consult the Suwannee River Wilderness Trail information provided by the State of Florida to tailor an experience that best meets your expectation and to avoid getting lost in the swamp as the author did back in the 1990s during a sixteen-mile solo paddle with no GPS available.

In keeping with some measure of geographic continuity, let's continue our trek south for an encounter with Tarzan just east of Ocala. No doubt that Johnny Weissmuller (aka Tarzan), having been raised in the surrounding jungle to live off the land, would have adapted well to the role of a pioneer paddler. A tour operator named Colonel Tooey on the Silver River decided to attempt to capitalize on the success of the 1930s film *Tarzan Finds A Son*, which was filmed in the area, and decided to release three male and three female Rhesus monkeys on an island in the river. The bungling businessman didn't

Pioneer Paddles of the Colonial South

A curious Rhesus on the Silver River

realize, however, that monkeys can swim. They quickly escaped the island and started breeding, leading to an estimated population of 1,000 descendants that roam the riverbank at present. Although an invasive species, wildlife biologists generally agree that the monkeys represent only a limited impact on the ecosystem and have become prey for foxes, owls, bobcats and alligators. We have paddled the area several times and counted as many as 38 monkeys on a day trip, including a mother Rhesus feeding her baby. To increase your sighting probability I would suggest choosing either an overcast day or launch during early morning or late afternoon.

William D. Auman

There is also a submerged dugout canoe near Geyser Spring that you can easily see on the white sandy bottom of the river. Begin your out-and-back trek at either Ray Wayside Park in Silver Springs or at Silver River State Park, but do take time to visit the state park's museum either way. One colonial-era highlight is to view the circa mid-1500s bronze Pedrero cannon on display, which was discovered nearby and was thought to have been made in Mexico under the watch of the infamous conquistador Hernan Cortes, known for his destruction of the Aztec Empire in Mexico. Neil Young describes how he came "dancing across the water with his galleons and guns" in his 1975 release entitled "Cortez the Killer," worthy of a listen. The museum also features a recovered cypress dugout canoe in case you miss the submerged one from your jungle trek.

Section Two: Manatees and Indian Royalty in the Nature/Sun Coast

The line where the Nature Coast gives way to the Sun Coast is not magically drawn on a latitude coordinate within Pasco County, where we spend the bulk of our time in the winter, yet the shores of the Gulf of Mexico *(apparently now known as the "Gulf of America" according to Google Maps and Donald Trump)* do generally transform from mangrove-dotted keys to the white, sandy beaches of Pinellas County that are flocked to each spring by a genre of snowbird known as a college student. Although those days are long in my rear view mirror, one of the rewards of the after-paddling experience is to visit what Pinellas has termed a "Gulp Coast" craft brewery.

Pioneer Paddles of the Colonial South

Jesus had his apostles and I have my "hopostle" card, which accompanies me as I spread the gospel of Madco Brewhouse (Madison County, NC's first brewery) often after a paddling adventure. The Indigenous Peoples of this region had their hemp (as did George Washington, who at one time was America's largest hemp farmer), but I'm not quite sure about their beer history. Archaeological evidence suggests that tribes may have used fermented beverages for ceremonial purposes and clearly the area pirates enjoyed their rum and grog, so perhaps one day I will discover a cache of such buried on an area key alongside a hoard of Spanish pieces of eight, doubloons and reales?

Pleasant day-dreams can always be revisited, but for now let's return to the water. The Pithlachascotee, or "Cotee" River as it is known locally, divides the towns of Port Richey and New Port Richey. Originating near Crews Lake, where cypress dugout canoes have been discovered, it flows south and west through the Starkey Wilderness Park before entering the Gulf at Miller's Bayou. On the south bank near the mouth of the river lies the well-preserved Olesner Mound, which landed on the National Register of Historic Places back in 2020. The grass and tree-covered rise holds tight to the secrets of a bygone era dating back to the Safety Harbor Period between 900 and 1400 A.D. Thought to have been utilized as a religious and ceremonial gathering place, Olesner has been remarkably preserved through the ages. An adjacent burial mound, however, was destroyed years ago due to commercial construction, which no doubt led to a curse inflicted upon those responsible.

There are many Cotee access areas in the vicinity of

William D. Auman

Millers Bayou, where the native chiefs surveyed the waters below their temple house. Nick's Waterfront Park in the restaurant district just across the bayou from the mound provides a public launch, as does Port Richey Waterfront Park just around the corner off of Old Post Road. Continue towards the Werner Salt Springs which begin only about a mile further north and you will find Brasher Park, yet another access point that can take you south towards the bayou, north towards Cow Key, or inland to explore the springs. Another popular option for paddling from Brasher would be to head out into the Gulf to Durney Key, which is roughly 2 miles off shore. A small island worthy of a stop for exploration and/or a swim, Durney Key sits among the historical "stilt houses" which were built between 1916 and 1918 on top of tall pilings. Originally built for use as fish camps, only eight of the original twenty-four remain due to the 1968 hurricane known as Gladys. Locals claim that part-time residents Johnny and June Carter Cash once owned one of the houses in addition to the residence that served as their winter home in Port Richey.

A paddle to Durney Key should only be undertaken on a calm-day, otherwise your paddling partner may become "slightly" disgruntled at the extra effort involved to avoid being swept away by the Gulf or perhaps even capsize, and she might even have a few foul words to express in your direction (yep, I couldn't make that one up). In order to avoid this and maintain marital bliss, on windy days choose to travel inland a few miles to the James Grey Preserve on the Cotee for a tranquil, calm and protected paddle, often complete with alligators to observe. Rest assured that these dinosaur-era creatures are more afraid of you than you are of them, just don't try to pet them. Look for them on a sunny day when the water is cool while they work on their tans

Pioneer Paddles of the Colonial South

along the river bank.

More local legends abound in this paddling paradise, which celebrates indigenous people every spring along the river with what is known as the Chasco Festival. Local folklore has it that a glazed clay container was discovered within the roots of a palm tree along the shore containing a parchment signed by Padre Luis, a Franciscan missionary of the order of St. Francis. The document, written in Castilian Spanish, tells the story of a DeValla, a Spanish nobleman who was charged by the King to subdue Indians in the area who had not converted to Christianity. During a subsequent battle near the mouth of the river, DeValla was slain along with all of his troops, however three civilians, including Dona Isabella, Phillip, and Padre Luis, were spared and began to live among the Native Americans.

After some time the chieftain, Mucoshee, adopted Dona as his daughter so that she could reign over the tribe as "Queen Chasco." He further declared Phillip to be "Prince Pithla" and the two were later married by Padre Luis. The tribe then lived in peace for many years. Fast forward to 1922 and the Chasco Fiesta of New Port Richey, now an annual event, was begun to honor the original inhabitants. No doubt that Mucoshee would be pleased that a river was later named for his son-in-law, yet the term "pithlo" is of Creek origin and translates into "canoe."

Continuing south from the mouth of the Cotee, options for mangrove-Gulf paddling are plentiful. Robert K. Rees Memorial Park at Green Key in New Port Richey offers a prime spot for a young kayaker to begin their lifetime of sea adventures with shallow sand flats along Big Bayou surrounding the causeway and protected island. Our oldest granddaughter Nyomi, age three at the time, counted eight dolphins on her maiden voyage from this locale. Eagle Point Park lies a few more miles south with options to venture into the Gulf at Fillman's Bayou or paddle inland on Trouble Creek. Chances are that you will see nesting bald eagles together with the common osprey and what our kids used to call the "flying dinosaur", aka the great blue heron. Yellow-crowned night herons together with little blue and green herons also make the area home with roseate spoonbill and wood stork sharing the neighborhood . Look closely into the water on a calm day and various type of rays and skates will likely be visible as well.

Follow along the Pasco Preserve that parallels the shoreline and you will soon reach Anclote Gulf Park. A consistent favorite trek is to put in adjacent to the pier and paddle north about a mile to the beaches of Key Vista Park, then upstream on Rocky Creek along the peninsula that we refer to as Gilligan's Island. Protected wilderness lines the Gulf shoreline throughout as I look for signs of either Mary Ann or Ginger. Take your canine and stop at one of many resting points for a swim or treasure hunt. Key Vista now features it's own modern launch as an option along the creek, which is only a short portage from the parking area.

Slightly south of Anclote Gulf Park lies Anclote River Park, known for its large Timucuan mound which is estimated to date back to the early 1200's. In the 1500's, Spanish explorers Vasco Da Gama and Alonso Alvarez de Pineda arrived in the area with their accompanying conquistadors. To navigate the shallow and meandering channels, they employed a kedge anchoring system, utilizing anchors at both the front and back of their ships. Ironically, the term Anclote translates into "tiny anchor."

On ancient maps, the little village of Anclote appears in 1545 where Native Americans had a large camp and burial grounds. Four additional mounds in the park were destroyed by irresponsible treasure hunters back in the 1950's, purportedly searching for booty believed to be buried in the area by the early 19th-century privateer Louis-Michel Aury. There is an episode of the History Channel's "Beyond Oak Island" series devoted to Aury's treasure and many theories abound as to where it may lie; maybe one day I'll get lucky and stumble upon it.

Just above the mouth of the Anclote and also marked within the park is the old Spanish Well, which according to legend was visited regularly by buccaneers who roamed the high seas to capture and pillage gold-laden vessels from England and Spain. Historians generally believe that Spanish invaders tortured the Timucuan into revealing the location of the well, which was one of the few sources of fresh water available for ships making the trip from the Gulf of Mexico to the Atlantic. Plans to further develop this park, which is already home to a large boat ramp, beach and bathhouses, were recently withdrawn due to local opposition. No doubt that further development would have adversely impacted the historical treasures believed to lie within the park's vicinity, so as John Lennon would say, chalk up a victory for power to the people! Once history is gone it cannot be replaced.

William D. Auman

Timucuan Mound circa 1200s on the Anclote River

    Although it is easy to drop a kayak at the river park and paddle either the mangrove shoreline or upstream toward the Sponge Docks of Tarpon Springs, another option can be found a few miles south at Fred Howard Park. A well-maintained kayak trail featuring a canopy of mangroves leads to a surreal experience as tunnels lead you through a maze of sub-tropical wilderness, only to emerge within view of the causeway and the greater Gulf. Turn north and paddle up the creek and you will soon reach Lake Avoca. Although some limited development appears along the north shore of the creek, it still lends toward a colonial-era experience.

Pioneer Paddles of the Colonial South

Before we leave the Anclote, consider a trek from the Tarpon Springs Splash Park, which offers the best of the 21st century as well as the 16th century all rolled into one. Take the kids and canine upstream for less than two miles on the Anclote to a sandy beach stop at Anclote Nature Park, a protected undeveloped reserve complete with trails to explore, then upon return you have modern-day options at both the splash park and the adjacent dog park.

A family that we recently met while putting in at Pop Stansell Park just south of Tarpon Springs in Palm Harbor had a different type of adventure in mind for the week. The young father, who had recently returned from being on the reality television show "Survivor", together with his wife and son, had just loaded two canoes full of firewood and other necessities that would sustain them for a week while camping on an uninhabited key within Sunderland Bayou. Many keys can be circumnavigated or explored from this convenient access point where one can time travel in a very quick and efficient manner. From the bayou you can see the Honeymoon Island Causeway to the south, which offers further convenient access to either the state park on the island or to Caladesi Island, an undeveloped gem along the sun coast just across St. Joseph's Sound from the park.

Although many paddle the relatively short trek to Honeymoon or Caladesi from the Dunedin Causeway, a lesser-known option can be found while launching from the south side of the causeway prior to the draw-bridge into North Clearwater Harbor. Less than a mile out you will find within the Pinellas Acquatic Preserve what was once known as NCH-13, a designated educational island with an easy landing point that includes a picnic table which seems to have come from out of nowhere since the island jungle is too thick to penetrate very far. I'm fairly certain that the Calusa did not build the picnic table, but since neither they nor the State of Florida have a formal name for NCH-13, I will christen it *Trouble Key* as of 2025 in honor of our Mini-Aussie who at age two had already been on over 50 kayaks trips as our first mate. If Donald Trump can rename the Gulf, I can certainly take the liberty of naming this uninhabited island after a worthy and loyal canine!

As we continue to work our way south some excellent paddling can be found in both Double Branch and Mobbly Bayou Preserves, each of which feature marked trails, great fishing (redfish, trout, snapper and even barracuda!) and an antidote recipe for those suffering from symptoms of wilderness solitude withdrawal. The area was once inhabited by Tocabaga Indians from approximately 900 A.D. until the 1500s, and they left multiple shell mounds behind that can still be seen today. Dolphins, manatees and otters are commonly encountered along the relatively easy out and back trails lined with wading birds that lead to the upper bay.

Adding to the abundance of historical paddles in the vicinity is Philippe Park in Safety Harbor, Follow the shoreline a short distance to view the largest remaining Tocabago Indian Mound in the Pinellas Peninsula. Records show that the same Pedro Menendez de Aviles who we encountered in St. Augustine actually visited the site in 1566 to help negotiate a peace treaty between the Tocabago and the Calusa Indians to the south. A conquistador brokering peace? That seems somewhat out of

Pioneer Paddles of the Colonial South

character, yet who am I to dispute the experts.

The historical legacy of the Tocabago goes much further than the Cigar City IPA that helped to put the Gulp Coast on the craft beverage map, with Weedon Island Preserve just off the south side of the Gandy bridge being perhaps the best place to experience their vast influence. Besides featuring a four-mile marked paddling trail that loops within the expansive preserve, the natural history center features a large collection of Native American artifacts including a 40-foot pine dugout canoe that was found within the preserve and thought to be roughly 1,100 years old. The makers of the canoe are thought to belong to the Manasota culture, a pre-historic ancestral tribe to the Tocabago, who left numerous shell middens within Tampa Bay.

Ironically, Tampa Bay was actually named by a Spanish historian who mistakenly believed that a Calusa Indian Village called *"Toempa"* was located in the bay area, although the Calusa's generally reigned in the region further south. Still, the name caught on as a replacement for the title of *"Bahia de Espiritu Santos,"* which had been bequeathed by none other than Hernando De Soto when he dropped by in 1539 to search for gold. Historians place his probable landfall to be close to the site of the engineering marvel known as the Sunshine Skyway bridge, which offers a nice bayside rest area on the southern side that can be utilized for yet another treasure-hunting paddling excursion into the Pinellas National Wildlife Refuge.

The Tampa Bay area actually became a hub for privateers working for the British during the post-Revolutionary period of 1799-1802 under a Loyalist named William Augustus

William D. Auman

Bowles, also known as *Estajoca*. Bowles attempted to form an independent state with the Muskogee (later known as the Seminole) and was authorized by Britain to issue letters of marque to ship captains, allowing them to legally attack Spanish ships. Bowles himself operated two schooners with a force of approximately 400 frontiersman, warriors and former slaves, but was captured in 1803 and died two years later in a Cuban prison, having starved himself to death as a final act of defiance.

No one has found any treasure attributable to Bowles, but just north of the Skyway a couple of pioneer paddles should not be missed. At Maximo Park a short paddle across Frenchman's Creek in Boca Ciega Bay allows for circumnavigation of Indian Key, where even more shell middens attributable to the Tocabago can be found. A prehistoric mound dating back approximately 10,000 years can also be seen within the park boundary. The park is ironically named for 1800s homesteader Antonio Maximo Hernandez, thought to be the first white settler on the peninsula, who was given a land grant for the property by virtue of his assistance to General Robert E. Lee during the Civil War.

Another option in the same vicinity is also worth the trip. Although some may define the term "colonial" somewhat differently than the author, Fort Desoto State Park does offer a Spanish-American War-era fort constructed between 1898-1906, not to mention a world-renowned beach located among a wealth of wildlife, birds, plants and sea life. Let's not forget the paddling trail that will take you along Mullet Key Bayou in the midst of protected, barrier island coastal wilderness, just as De Soto would have experienced centuries earlier.

Pioneer Paddles of the Colonial South

Before we leave the Sun Coast, let's geographically zigzag slightly north and inland to the Hillsborough River. It's hard to fathom that this meandering, spring-fed river that originates in the Green Swamp is the same that ends its journey in the metropolis of Tampa some 54 miles downstream, but it is well-deserving of the designated paddling trail that bears its name. There are a total of nine access points within the 30-mile trail with varying degrees of difficulty, so be sure to check out the trail guide online before embarking. Rowlett Park at the southern terminus of the trail is a favorite that allows for a scenic paddle with little tidal influence after putting in below the dam.

Hillsborough River State Park marks the beginning of the trail and features a replica of Fort Foster, originally built in 1836 during the Second Seminole War to safeguard the bridge that carried Fort King Road across the river. The paddling route south essentially parallels the road, which formerly served as the main transportation route between Fort Brooke in Tampa and Fort King in Ocala and was believed to be part of the route taken by De Soto on his expedition in the 1540s. In 1835, Seminole warriors ambushed Major Francis Dade's detachment along the road further north as they were attempting to enforce a controversial treaty to remove the tribe.

The three-mile stretch that ends at Dead River Park is one not to be missed for colonial paddling purposes. Hit your time travel button and enjoy the aura of a wilderness preserve that no doubt looks much as it did when the Seminole called the area home. Chances are good that you will be joined by a lazy 'gator or two sunning themselves along the bank, so leave Fido at home and be cautious if you decide to take a dip to cool off.

William D. Auman

Section Three: A Paradise Coast, a River of Grass and America's Caribbean

Unbeknownst to many, including myself until recently, the Caribbean Ecological Division encompasses southern Florida from the Everglades southward all the way to Key West. Accordingly, our country is considered to be one of boundary nations of the Caribbean Sea. I must admit, the luminescent aqua water that begins in Key Largo does resemble that found along the colonial buccaneer havens of Port Royal or Nassau, but differs considerably from that which Marjory Stoneman Douglas coined the "river of grass" back in 1947, aka the Everglades. The ever-so slow movement of shallow sheetflow through the sawgrass marshes lends to blackish hues as the water enters into places such as Hells Half Acre or Glades Haven.

The Paradise Coast of the southwestern peninsula has more translucent tones of a greenish blue, but is also burdened with a post-colonial migration of invading humans known as "snowbirds" that have paved much of paradise to put up parking lots (revisiting Joni Mitchell). Although not as populous as the southeastern coast, much has changed since I first began canoeing this area back in the early 1980s. The devastation of 2022's Hurricane Ian has led to an influx of even more building and re-building, yet some pioneer paddling opportunities still remain in what was the land of the mighty Calusa.

The Calusa empire controlled most of South Florida long before Bahamian or Spanish explorers ever showed up. They lived on the coastal waterways with homes built on stilts in a time before FEMA required such for building code purposes. Their peak population has been estimated to be around 50,000 and remnants of their shell mounds can be found along a multitude of creeks, streams and mangrove islands throughout the region. Pine Island is virtually inundated with these mounds, with several homes in the Pineland area on the north side having been built on top of these ancient mounds before regulations prohibited the practice. It is easy to launch along the shoreline and paddle out about a mile to Black Key in the Pine Island Sound Aquatic Preserve or north along the shoreline to Big Jim Creek Preserve.

Sanibel and Captiva Islands both offer similar opportunities to experience a piece of our remaining mangrove wilderness, The former features the J.N. "Ding" Darling National Wildlife Refuge, a popular bird watching destination with paddling permitted through the tidal flats on the right side of the roughly 4.5 mile wildlife drive. Sanibel also offers the 2.5 mile Commodore Creek Paddling Trail, a loop which begins about a half-mile from the launch on Tarpon Bay. A total of 17 markers will help you stay on course while you explore the many mangrove tunnels.

A similar loop trail of four miles can be found on Captiva Island adjacent to Sanibel in area known as Buck Key, just watch out for raccoons that may cross over your head when paddling through a mangrove tunnel. Our kids were glad that a rascally raccoon didn't fall into our canoe when he decided to surprise us while our attention was focused on one of the numerous shell middens that lie alongside the trail. Those ancient artifacts date back as much as 2,500 years.

Juan Ponce de Leon is believed to have discovered Sanibel and Captiva back in 1513 while searching for his fountain of youth, naming the former "Santa Isybella" after then Spanish Queen Isabella. He and his fellow conquistadors battled the Calusa for years, and Ponce eventually suffered an ultimately fatal arrow attack at their hands in 1523. Rumors abound as to how the Calusa would execute or hold for ransom Spanish prisoners and shipwreck victims, but local legend also attributes this to the infamous (but arguably fictitious) pirate known as Jose Gaspar. Gaspar supposedly buried his treasure on Sanibel and subsequently built a prison on "Isle de los Captivas." Gaspar was allegedly captured by the U.S. Navy in 1821, but wrapped himself in chains and jumped overboard off of his ship rather than face imprisonment. I'm still looking for his purported treasure, but have yet to experience any ghostly apparitions that could serve as a clue to its whereabouts. Perhaps I should try a full moon paddle or some form of séance?

Close by we find Matlacha, known as America's "fishingist" village, which sits on a man-made island between the mainland and Pine Island. It's hard to believe, but Matlacha was created in 1926 by the dredging up of oyster beds. You can circumnavigate the small island or simply explore the creeks along the shoreline of the Matlacha Pass Aquatic Preserve, where you will often be joined by curious dolphins. The first settlers on the island, which the Calusa never saw, were actually squatters who were depression-era refugees. You can launch from the island park or at Sirenia Vista access, which is just across Buzzard Bay on the Cape Coral side of the mainland.

Pioneer Paddles of the Colonial South

Whereas shell mounds may be lacking on Matlacha, a unique one known as "Mound House" can be visited or paddled past on Estero Bay at Ft. Myers Beach. This oldest house on the beach was built on top of a 2,000 year-old Calusa mound in 1906, however the mound was partially destroyed in the 1950s when new owners decided to install an in-ground swimming pool. Thankfully, the structure was eventually purchased by the town and restored to be a protected archaeological site. If paddling to the site, beware the many powerboats and jet skis that continually serve to remind us that we are actually in the 21st century.

Bunche Beach Preserve along San Carlos Bay lends to a more colonial aura with its 718 acres of protected forest and coastline. Named for Dr. Ralph Bunche, the first black American Nobel Peace Prize recipient, during segregation it was the only beach that black people could visit in the area. A kayak launch allows for a paddle out Rock Creek into the bay, where you can turn north to explore undeveloped Plover Island, a hidden gem off the beaten track. Again, be cautious of tidal impacts as low tide could result in water depths of only an inch or two along the salt flats.

Although the Fort Myers/Cape Coral area is brimming with traffic and fellow humans, there are a few enduring urban area treks worth taking. The Orange River canoe access, although next to a power plant, is an urban delight for those who want a quick respite from their daily grind. The plant, which lies adjacent to Manatee Park, provides warm water discharge that creates a natural spa for the locally resident manatees when the Gulf temperatures drop below 68 degrees. Further north,

William D. Auman

Telegraph Creek Preserve near Alva contains 1,730 acres of wilderness and is next door to the 5,620 acre Bob James Preserve, which is, in turn, adjacent to the 67,619 acre Babcock Ranch Preserve. Launch off of North River Road and be prepared to view this part of Florida in an environment similar to what the conquistadors must have seen. Uncrowded and scenic,

Plover Island adjoins San Carlos Bay and overlooks Sanibel Island

the preserve is home to wildlife including the endangered black panther, although I have yet to make their acquaintance. Don't be surprised, however, if you happen to see a camel or other non-native beastly resident since the route takes you by an exotic animal farm.

Returning to the city, Four-Mile Cove Ecological

Pioneer Paddles of the Colonial South

Preserve, aka "Eco Park", can be found just north of the Veteran's Parkway Bridge that connects Fort Myers to Cape Coral. Consisting of 365 undeveloped acres with more soon to be added, an urban wilderness paddle through the saltwater marsh, mangrove swamp and cabbage palm hammocks can take you quickly back to an earlier time. Deerfly Creek, 4-Mile Creek and a variety of inlets within the preserve that connect to the Caloosahatchee River are ripe for exploration.

Each of the above southwestern coastal paddles are part of the Great Calusa Blueway, a joint venture between Lee County Parks and Recreation and their Visitor and Convention Bureau. Divided into three regions: Estero Bay, Pine Island Sound and the Caloosahatchee River, the Blueway offers meticulous resources for exploration of its 190 miles of bays and rivers, many of which still resonate with a colonial-era vibe. Before leaving the area I must mention one additional highlight, that being Lover's Key, a wilderness paddling paradise located between Estero Bay and the Gulf of Mexico. As late as the early 1900s these barrier islands were accessible only by boat, and it was said that only lovers made the effort to get to this romantic destination, which saw its first road built in 1965. On a calm day you may opt for open water, but there is a five-mile loop trial along the creeks within the park that is conducive to a time-traveling experience.

Local legend claims that Black Island within Lovers Key got its name from Black Augustus, a pirate who had escaped capture and made this island home for the remainder of his life. A Portuguese private allegedly under Jose Gaspar, in 1821 he escaped an attack by American forces and sailed south to the island, where he lived as a recluse until he died in the 1870s. Augustus was known only to some local fisherman with whom he traded, including John Butterfield who lived on Mound Key at the time. Soon after Augustus passed, Butterfield built a new store, a new home, sent his daughter to college and bought his wife an organ. I'm guessing that someone may have found pirate treasure?

When pioneer paddling the southwestern Gulf, don't neglect to consider the Upper Manatee River and Little Manatee River, each of which has its own designated paddling trail that is easy to download. The Manatee River is often called the "Singing River" due to a Native American legend that describes how the river mysteriously makes music on certain moons, so listen closely. Not to forget, when rambling down towards Everglades City, don't bypass the Blackwater River in the Big Cypress Preserve. During the Third Seminole War, the Seminoles retreated into this area while hiding from the soldiers who continued to search for them. One crude military map from 1857 illustrates the Blackwater River and an area labeled "palm grove", which is now part of Collier-Seminole State Park and contains a stand of beautiful royal palms. There is a 13.6 mile paddling trail within the park that is influenced heavily by tides, but allows for a shorter out-and-back option. The northern islands of the Ten Thousand Islands National Wildlife Refuge lie just off shore for those adventurous souls who want to decompress further from the 21st century rat race and spend a few days camping and island-hopping throughout the 35,000 acres of winding waterways.

Continuing south, wilderness waterway adventures

abound where Big Cypress National Preserve and Everglades National Park share a common border, but you will need the bug spray even during the winter months. The fresh waters of the 729,000 acre Big Cypress are essential to the health of the neighboring Everglades, the largest UNESCO-designated sub-tropical wilderness reserve on the North American continent, which encompasses more than 4,300 square miles of southern Florida. At one point the shallow, slow-moving sheets of water flowed freely southward from the Kissimmee River and covered roughly 11,000 square miles, but by the early 1900s development began to severely transform the ecosystem and the species that it supported. Thank goodness that the park was established in 1947 to conserve the natural landscape and prevent further degradation of the environment.

Obviously, the Calusa were the earliest documented inhabitants of the region, maintaining a highly organized society that left behind many traces of their civilization from shell works and tools to long distance canoe trails. After the Spanish arrived in 1513, the tribal population was decimated through war and incoming disease brought by settlers. The influx of settlement to the north later resulted in the arrival of the Seminole and Miccosukee, who still inhabit the area today along with the co-existing alligators and crocodiles.

Others also called the 'glades home prior to creation of the park, included rum-runners, pot smugglers, whiskey distillers and many other nefarious characters, to go along with many families who adapted to the environment and lived off the land. Rumor has it that Confederate soldiers buried a treasure trove of gold near an abandoned Seminole Village deep in the swamp, but it has yet to be found. Known as Lost City and about eight miles south of Alligator Alley, some further claim that Al Capone used the village site to produce moonshine in the 1930s.

A "friendly" Crocodile and 'Gator on the Turner River in the Everglades

On one of my many canoe trips across Chokoloskee Bay during the early 1980s era of Ronald Reagan, this somewhat nefarious character decided to launch next to a "no trespassing" sign that had been temporarily installed due to the government having been shut down. As I told the other two canoeists who soon followed my lead, Woody Guthrie said that the other side of that sign, which said nothing, was the side that was made for you and me. This land is your land, this land is my land...and it was made for you and me. Although I admit to having joined the ranks of those who may purportedly have run afoul of the law, I did manage to make a clean getaway and the statute of limitations on the misdemeanor has now run!

Adjacent to Everglades City, it is easy to launch from Chokoloskee Island and venture out into the southern keys of the Ten Thousand Islands National Wildlife Refuge, just make note of your route and take your GPS. The islands are actually islets, very small mangrove keys that grow on top of oyster bars with much of their landmass just above the waterline, but there are many and it is relatively easy to get disoriented. Some area guides claim that the actual number of islands is actually in the 14,000-16,000 range, so it may be more difficult than one may think to locate and rescue Gilligan without some measure of 21st century technology to assist navigation.

Another option would be the Halfway Creek paddling trail, a well-marked scenic waterway that can be done either out-and-back or with the addition of a loop that includes the Barron River. The more adventurous could make it an entire day trip and take out in Everglades City. There is an easy free launch site behind the Big Cypress Welcome Center on the Tamiami Trail that can transport you quickly into a colonial mindset that is only occasionally interrupted by the sound of an airboat in the distance. Water levels are generally good throughout the year, as opposed to the Turner River which also has a nearby Tamiami Trail launch site. Check the water levels at the visitor center before choosing the Turner option, which is 8.5 miles to Chokoloskee unless you opt for an out-and-back. Keep in mind that chances of seeing an alligator on either of these treks are very high and the chance of seeing Florida's unofficial state insect, the mosquito, are even higher!

William D. Auman

The wilderness of the Everglades is mystical. One can only imagine what it was like in the days before development changed the landscape. As we continue east towards the American Caribbean, we should take a moment to appreciate this living, breathing, testament to nature in its most resilient and magical form.

The Florida Keys, a chain of over 800 tropical islands stretching some 180 miles, are home to a multitude of pioneer-style paddling opportunities that I will continue to discover as long as I am physically able to do so. With that being said, I again emphasize the disclaimer that this is not intended to be a comprehensive treatise of recommendations and my apologies to the bodies of water that did not make their way onto the printed pages. The same can be said for portions of the southeastern coast and panhandle, areas that I also aim to explore further as time goes by. For now, I must conclude this chapter with some worthy Caribbean-style highlights that the time-traveler should not miss.

Ponce de Leon sailed by the Keys in 1513 and named them *Los Martires* (the Martyrs), supposedly because the profiles of the islands looked to him as being twisted and tormented. It is possible, albeit not historically documented, that he made landfall here before continuing north. If so, that would make him the first European to set foot in the Keys.

Key Largo, the northernmost major island in the chain, is rightfully known as the snorkeling capital of the United States with its close proximity to the third-largest coral reef system in the world, found off its eastern coast in the Atlantic Ocean. It is

Pioneer Paddles of the Colonial South

easy to kayak either the Atlantic or Gulf shorelines of the island depending upon surf, tide and wind conditions. As with the other keys, these islands can serve as a barrier to enable leeward-side paddling opportunities on gusty days. Keep in mind that pollution, over-fishing and climate change have all impacted the ecosystem of the area and we should all do our part as conservationists to minimize further impacts. Marine biologists estimate that roughly 90% of corals within the reefs have been lost in the last 40 years alone; sad but true.

A favorite spot for a colonial adventure lies within John Pennekamp State Park. Although it is possible to paddle out into the Atlantic to one of three reef systems, the closest of which is about 300 yards offshore, we prefer the mangrove trails that meander from the launch on Largo Sound along the creeks that lie within the vast sanctuary. Approximately 178 nautical square miles of coral reefs, seagrass beds and mangrove swamp are beckoning for exploration. You can paddle past and on a calm day actually see submerged artifacts, including a cannon and anchor from a 1715 Spanish shipwreck, that were placed about 100 yards off of Cannon Beach back in the 1970s.

Perhaps more in tune with the scuba-diver due to the swift currents that can challenge a kayak, within the Florida Keys National Marine Sanctuary lies a trail of nine historic shipwrecks for potential exploration. The oldest wreck on the trail is the *San Pedro* from 1733, a member of the Spanish treasure fleet that was caught in a hurricane and sank about a mile south of Indian Key. While intriguing and worthy of mention, someone else will need to write about pioneer diving the colonial south.

William D. Auman

Numerous access points can be explored through online resources and also seen by simply driving down US 1, the Overseas Highway now known as Jimmy Buffett Memorial Highway after the iconic musician, writer and humanitarian. Many times we have come upon a place to launch that has led to a recapture of that time-traveling mindset that one cultivates through communion with remaining coastal wilderness. Indian Key Historic State Park is one such destination, located less than a mile offshore at mile-marker 78.5 just off Lower Matacumbe Key. As of this writing, the access ramp at Indian Key Fill is closed for repair, but you can opt to launch on the opposite side of US 1 for a short paddle through the Lignumvitae Key Aquatic Preserve and go under the bridge at Indian Key Channel in order to head into the Atlantic. Jacob Housman, a shipwreck salvage tycoon of sorts, bought the key in 1831 and ultimately had it declared as the first county seat for what was then Dade County. In 1840, Seminole Indians attacked the island which was known for its well-stocked store, killing many inhabitants. Accessible only by boat, the uninhabited park was placed on the National Register of Historic Places in 1972.

Other favorites include Long Key Lake at the state park of the same name, an area settled initially by the Tequesta, a small tribe of Native Americans that eventually succumbed to the mighty Calusa and are largely overlooked today in popular accounts of colonial history. Archaeologists generally agree that the Tequesta dug a canoe channel from Long Key Lake to the Atlantic which was later used by the Calusa. Many years of environmental impact has reclaimed the channel, yet the lake makes for a tranquil paddling experience. Atlantic shoreline access is also easy at the beach area of the park.

Pioneer Paddles of the Colonial South

A few miles southward we reach Vaca Key and Curry Hammock State Park, which features a 1.5 mile loop trail around Little Crawl Key, complete with mangrove tunnels and a deep water lagoon. You can extend the trip to 5 miles if you choose to circumnavigate Deer Key just off the coast. The access area at Coco Plum Park just south of Curry Hammock is another viable option and allows for a short paddle north into a protected shoreline with numerous sandy driftwood beaches to explore. The first historical mention of Key Vaca is its appearance on a Spanish map in the 1500s. About 50 years after Columbus' first voyage, a young Spanish sailor by the name of Hernando Escalante Fontanada was shipwrecked near "Cayo Vaca" and captured by the Indians who lived there. After eighteen years in captivity, he was freed and returned to Spain where he wrote an account of his experiences on the island.

Opposite from Coco Plum and Curry Hammock on the Gulf side of America's Caribbean is little-known Sunset Bay Park on Grassy Key, which has a small beach for easy access. Just follow Kyle Avenue off of the Overseas Highway and when it ends take a left on Morton Street. A paddle to the south takes you to Crawl Key and then Long Point Key, or you can follow the Grassy Key shoreline north for an easy out-and-back. An even lesser-known launching pad can be found at the end of 61st street in Marathon, just stay off the private property that abuts close to each side of the barricade. From here it is about a mile to circumnavigate protected Rachel Key just off of Crane Point Hammock, which is laden with multitudes of seabirds.

Calusa history abounds in this area, particularly at Boot Key which lies within the city of Marathon and is thought to be the site of one of their villages from the 15th through 17th centuries. Disconnected from the city by a bridge that was closed in 2010 and once slated for development, Boot Key features a pristine mangrove swamp with lagoons and unmarked narrow mangrove tunnels that are best traversed at higher tides. Put in adjacent to the pier at Sombrero Beach along Sister Creek and keep to the left as you enter the protected wilderness area that leads to the lagoon entrance on the back side. There is also trail access just across Sister Creek from the launch for a short trek option.

  Perhaps our premier favorite paddling spot in the keys appears just south of the modern-day Seven Mile Bridge, representing the sequel to the one constructed for what was then known as the Overseas Railroad from 1909 to 1912 under the direction of Henry Flagler. A diamond in a land of emeralds, Bahia Honda Key is actually a prehistoric coral reef that emerged due to a drop in sea level several thousand years ago. Consider wind and tide before opting for either a pristine Atlantic shoreline paddle among coastal hardwood hammocks or Gulf-side access from the deep water lagoon where dolphins often frolic. An undeveloped peninsula with private beach areas to pick from is within easy reach of the Gulf launch.

Pioneer Paddles of the Colonial South

The tranquil beauty of Bahia Honda Key

Further south near Mile Marker 25 we find the remote access of Niles Road Beach. With virtually no development in any direction, this area has largely remained much as it was when the Calusa empire was king. For a short family trip, paddle about a half mile north to a landing area that can also be hiked to from the access area. It is easy to lengthen your trek by circumnavigating Key Who to the southeast, or venture further to Knockendown Key through the many mangrove tunnels that propagate the area. Big Torch Key is to the north is another option for a seemingly endless tropical wilderness experience.

William D. Auman

  So now we can continue on to the end of US 1 for about a half-hour (by car, not kayak) and celebrate at Captain Tony's in Key West! Originally an ice house that doubled as the city morgue when it was constructed back in 1851, it later morphed into a cigar factory and later a bordello. In 1933, a local named Josie Russell bought what was then a speakeasy and created the original Sloppy Joe's, who name was suggested by Russell's close friend, a guy named Ernest Hemingway. "Papa" Hemingway, Tennessee Williams, and Jimmy Buffett were all frequent patrons of what later became Captain Tony's when charter boat captain Tony Tarracino bought the bar in 1968.. Papa was not only an iconic author, but also an accomplished fisherman. I'm not sure if he canoed back in the day, but it is easy to imagine *The Old Man in the Sea* as being quite an accomplished paddler. The vibe of Key West is addictive and the people quite diverse and independent. In 1982 they deemed themselves the "Conch Republic" and declared secession from the Union in protest of a U.S. Border Patrol blockade that allowed for unlawful searches during the "war on drugs." The name stuck.

  You can paddle Key West just as easily as every other island in the chain, but colonial enthusiasts should definitely visit the Mel Fisher Museum, home to the treasures found from Spanish galleons *Nuestra Senora de Atocha* and artifacts from the slave ship *Henrietta Marie*. The *Atocha*, having sunk near Key West during a hurricane in 1622, was discovered by Fisher in 1985, together with an estimated cache of $450 million, including 40 tons of gold and silver, 114,000 Spanish silver pieces of eight (yep, my wife even bought one for me!), numerous Columbian emeralds, and 1,000 silver ingots. Fisher

Pioneer Paddles of the Colonial South

had previously discovered the *Marie* back in 1972 which searching for the *Atocha,* and salvaged two anchors, a cannon, the 1699 bronze ship's bell, and some 30,000+ glass beads. It had wrecked approximately 35 miles west of Key West in 1700 after leaving Port Royal, Jamaica.

Port Royal was a pirate haven and frequented by many swashbucklers including Blackbeard, aka Edward Teach, who was known to frequent Key West when away from his adopted home in North Carolina. A whole book could easily be devoted to the illustrious history of the keys and the paddling destinations that can creatively teleport the paddler back to the time of the Calusa, conquistadors and buccaneers, but it is time to move on within the south to my native Old North State and tell a few tales of Blackbeard, Daniel Boone and others.

William D. Auman

CHAPTER TWO

NORTH CAROLINA: Sir Walter Raleigh to the Appalachians

Section One: Searching for a Lost Colony

When exploring coastal North Carolina it is important to channel the spirit of John Lawson, the infamous English explorer and historian who set sail to the Carolinas in August of 1700 to assume appointment as Surveyor-General of North Carolina. At that time the Carolina swamps and backcountry were essentially unknown and forbidding destinations, but remnants of those habitats can still be encountered today. Lawson documents his discoveries in *A New Voyage to Carolina,* first published in 1709, but his journeys never reached beyond our piedmont region and he never met Daniel Boone, who began his frontier career after his family moved to Dutchman's Creek along the Yadkin River back in 1753. On a side note, I can claim that Boone's family were ancestral neighbors since they, like my family, migrated down the Great Wagon road from the Reading, Pennsylvania area to North Carolina, although my direct ancestor came a few years later--1791 to be exact. Yes, I have a muzzle-loading Kentucky rifle and a 'coonskin cap that I wear when I visit my psychologist.

Before we venture west, however, let's time travel into the coastal region of the Old North State, which is rich in history and laden with golden opportunities to paddle into Neverland.

Pioneer Paddles of the Colonial South

The English exploration of our seaboard began with the Fort Raleigh expedition, which later set the stage for what became to be known as the Lost Colony. In 1584, Captains Philip Amadas and Arthur Barlowe arrived just north of Roanoke Island and befriended Granganimeo, the brother of Wingina, who was the tribal chief of the local Indigenous Peoples. They traded with the Indians and later returned to England with two members of the Roanoke tribe, Wanchese and Manteo, and reported to their benefactor, Sir Walter Raleigh, of a prosperous and fruitful land. This led to a second voyage in 1585 of seven ships under the command of Sir Richard Grenville, Raleigh's cousin, with 500 men who built a fort on the island. This time, however, relations with Wingina deteriorated, battles ensued, winter came and the renowned privateer Sir Francis Drake fortuitously happened along to rescue the starving men and return them to England. Fifteen men were left behind to guard the fort.

In 1587, Raleigh decided to try a different approach, an agrarian-based colony as opposed to militaristic. 110 colonists, including 17 women and 9 children, soon arrived back on Roanoke under the leadership of their appointed governor, John White, only to find that the remaining soldiers had been killed. White, an artist by profession, subsequently left in pictures and text the first depictions of our country's east coast wilderness areas. All surviving original drawings are showcased at the print room of the British Museum in London, but can be accessed online thanks to an agreement with the staff of *Virtual Jamestown*. My personal favorite is the watercolor entitled "Indians Fishing" that shows native Secotan Indians, thought to be of the Algonquin Nation, paddling their cypress dugout canoes along the sound.

William D. Auman

Returning to the story, Governor White soon departed for England to obtain additional supplies. Unfortunately, war had broken out with Spain and his return to Roanoke was delayed for three years. When he finally arrived back in Roanoke there were no settlers to be found. He saw no sign of violence, fortifications and homes were intact, but his family and the other settlers were missing. His only clue was the word CROATOAN carved into a tree and CRO carved into another that stood nearby.

The story of the Lost Colony is one that pervades western civilization classes from elementary school through advanced graduate study. Although Roanoke Island has endured over four centuries of change since the disappearance of the settlers, it is still possible to envision the environment within which these brave individuals attempted to gain a foothold. Paddle along the waterfront of Manteo *(*named in honor of the Algonquian Indian who befriended the settlers and was later baptized as the Lord of Roanoke on August 27, 1587)* in Shallowbag Bay and you will see the Elizabeth II, a replica of one of the three ships that brought the lost colonists to the island. There is an easy access launch at the end of Queen Elizabeth Street across from Festival Island. Paddle on the north end of Roanoke and living history continues in a less cosmopolitan setting and where you will find the remains of Fort Raleigh.

This "New Forte in Virgina" is the only structure connected to the Lost Colony whose site has been exactly located through the efforts of extensive excavations beginning in 1936. The national historic site can be viewed by kayak or canoe from Roanoke Sound, and hiking trails through a quiet wooded area lead to the site and the breathtaking Elizabethan Gardens.

Pioneer Paddles of the Colonial South

  Theories abound as to what happened to the settlement, which included young Virginia Dare, known to all as White's granddaughter and the first child born of English parents in the New World on August 20, 1587. Perhaps some modern day paddler will happen along some additional item of archaeological evidence and help supply a piece of the ancient

The Elizabeth II at anchor in Manteo echoes remembrance of a colony that vanished

puzzle? Recent discoveries of European artifacts at an inland site approximately fifty miles from the colony near the confluence of Salmon Creek and the Albermarle Sound have been cited as evidence that a group of survivors may have settled there. This area appears as Site "X" on White's map *La Virginiea Pars,* and is situated next to a Weapemoc Indian village known as Mettaquem.

Put in at the the US 17 bridge just east of Midway before the Chowan River and it is an approximate 3.5 mile paddle to the mouth of the creek. You will be surrounded by 1,000 protected acres of the Salmon Creek State Natural Area along the way, a surreal experience among the spirits of the Weapemoc.

Roanoke Island was not only home to John White's village of mystery, but also to the Freedman's Colony, a haven for runaway slaves during the Civil War. The island served as host to a battle between the Union and Confederacy, and remnants of forts from that era can still be seen on the western side of the island. Begin your trek at the public ramp at the end of Bowser Town Road and paddle north for a day trip that will take you not only on a voyage through history but also to the state aquarium, a destination that can cause adults to become kids again (**Editors note: North Carolina is home to two additional coastal aquariums, located at Pine Knoll Shores and Fort Fisher)*.

After experiencing the jewel that is Roanoke, cross over the bridge and head toward Kitty Hawk along US 158. You may wish to stop off for a hike or paddle along the sound adjacent to Nags Head Woods at Kill Devil Hills, or you may prefer the narrow waterway that appears just before reaching the Wright Memorial Bridge. Known as Jean Guite Creek, it is easy to launch and leave civilization behind as you paddle north towards

Pioneer Paddles of the Colonial South

Southern Shores accompanied by otters, herons, egrets, and a variety of reptiles. Giant crepe myrtle trees provide a canopy along the 3.6 mile out-and-back route which adjoins the Kitty Hawk Forest Preserve.

If you would rather take a southern route and begin the trek towards Ocracoke, the Pea Island Wildlife Refuge offers natural habitats to explore. The refuge is located on Hatteras Island and extends from Oregon Inlet south to the village of Rodanthe. Just follow NC 12 and you will pass several parking areas with trail and/or boat access. Ocean beaches, barrier dunes, salt marshes, fresh and brackish water ponds, tidal creeks, and bays can all be found within the boundaries of this contemporary Eden, but the crown jewel may be the 25,700 acres of Pamlico Sound waters. Snow geese, tundra swans, bald eagles and peregrine falcons are but a few of the migratory waterfowl and raptors who call this area on the Atlantic Flyway a temporary home.

Just south of Eagle Nest Bay paddlers will thrill to the natural beauty and mesmerizing sunsets on the waters of North Pond, North Field Pond, and South Pond. You would think that the powers that be could have come up with more unique names for these picturesque remnants of coastal wilderness. Why not Sir Francis Pond? Peregrine Field? Oh well, maybe those aren't much better after all. New Inlet, just past the visitor station on highway 12, also affords a great spot to launch your canoe or kayak into Pamlico Sound.

The Pea Island area is thought to be the locale where Sir Walter Raleigh (yep, same guy), sent a small exploring expedition a few years prior to his colonizing efforts. The story goes that on the third day of their stay on what was then known as Hatarask Island, three Indians in a canoe appeared. They seemed afraid of the giant ship and the strange beings inside it, but the Englishmen persuaded one of them to come aboard. He was promptly given a shirt, hat, and a few drinks of wine. Wine in lieu of rum? Something must be wrong here, but it worked out just the same. The native soon returned with a load of fish from his dugout for the Europeans. This led to a visit from the chief's brother, Granganimeo, and a friendship that at least initially was more genuine than that enjoyed by the Pilgrims to the north. It further served as an impetus for the Fort Raleigh expedition.

How delightful it is to be able to see this area in a form similar to what it must have resembled over 400 years ago! No condominiums, no roller coasters, just solitude and shipwrecks in the surf and beyond. Several parking areas off of highway 12 will house your vehicle as you put in to paddle the *Graveyard of the Atlantic*. From 1650 through 1850 over 2,000 ships found their way to the bottom of the ocean thanks to North Carolina's dreaded shoals and shifting sand bars, hence the name. Keep in mind that this is a barrier island, and in the warmer months it shares the trademark weather patterns of the tropics, i.e. thunderstorms and riptide currents. Although shoals and sand bars don't generally serve as hazards for the paddler, the surf can be dangerous. Accordingly, be aware of any advisories and take necessary precautions.

The Cape Hatteras National Seashore is a national treasure and one of the many natural areas that make our state so

Pioneer Paddles of the Colonial South

unique for many outdoor activities. Books can be and have been written about this area alone, so I will leave you to consult with them and take our boats further south for another segment of coastal exploration.

Section Two: Paddling in Blackbeard's Wake

"Only the devil and I know the whereabouts of my treasure, and the one of us who lives the longest should take it all!"
Edward Teach

William D. Auman

I am often asked why the infatuation with pirate history? Answers are not very difficult—admiration of a swashbuckling adventuring spirit, treasure hunting, enjoying aspects of the plunder obtained while toasting a mug full of grog, etc. Sure, some buccaneers were arguably "criminal" by historical and contemporary standards, yet they were also among the most inclusive and democratic entities that existed during the "pioneer" age. Some exhibited a "Robin Hood-esq" persona, as in take from the rich and spread the wealth among the poor. They were generally inclusive, with a typical pirate crew consisting of an unorthodox mix of sailors, escaped convicts, former slaves and other men disillusioned with societal norms, all of whom were required to honor a code of articles that limited their captain's power with adherence to a democratic system of government.

By way of background, some of the first indigenous peoples to interact with "Pyrates" included the Pasquotank, Chowan, Pamlico, Tuscarora and Roanoke. These names resonate in contemporary society as designations for cities, counties, rivers, lakes and sounds. One of the most beautiful islands in the world holds claim to a tribal namesake of Algonquian origin, that being Ocracoke. It is designated on an early map drawn by John White in 1585 as *Woccocock*, and sometimes appears on other maps as being *Wocon*, or *Wokokin*. Ironically, one of the most famous from the Golden Age of Piracy was actually a part-time resident of North Carolina who was extra-judicially hunted down and executed off the island of Ocracoke. You may know him as Blackbeard.

A popular local story attributes the naming of Ocracoke

Pioneer Paddles of the Colonial South

to Blackbeard from the year 1718. The impatient pirate captain walked the deck of his ship all night while waiting for the onset signal of what was to become the Battle of Ocracoke Inlet. He knew when the cock first crowed that action would begin and suddenly cried out "O Crow Cock!" several times. Had he known that this morning of battle would be his last, perhaps he would have not been so inclined to rush the issue!

I doubt that Captain Edward Teach *(aka Edward Thatch, aka Blackbeard)*, had any idea that the morning of November 22, 1718, would end with his severed head being strapped to the bow pulpit of the invading sloop of Virginia's Lt. Robert Maynard. Accordingly, he probably did not name the island of Ocracoke. In fact, he and his remaining crew on the *Adventure,* the ship of which he received vested title from the vice-admiralty court in Bath, were probably quite hung over from their final beach blast of grog at Springer's Point the night before. Maynard had been sent by Governor Alexander Spotswood of Virginia, uninvited, to encroach upon the colony of Carolina and kill the pirate, who had recently received a pardon from his part-time neighbor, Governor Charles Eden. To make a long story short, Blackbeard succumbed to his assassins from the Royal Navy in hand-to-hand combat after being shot a total of five times and stabbed at least twenty. His headless body supposedly swam around Maynard's sloop three times before sinking into Teach's Hole.

Teach's Hole is the local name for the sound side of the southern tip of Ocracoke Island, just off Springer's Point, which is the highest point on the island and marked by its rocky shoreline. Legend has it that the pirate crew enjoyed quite a party at that venue during the evening prior to Maynard's attack. After taking the ferry from either Cedar Island, Swan Quarter, or Hatteras (the free one), put your canoe or kayak into Silver Lake Harbor and turn left as you paddle through the "Ditch" just next to the National Park Service Visitor Center. In less than a mile you will see the point and sandy beach, which is a great spot for a picnic lunch or bottle of rum if you are feeling pyrated. Take time to scan the trails, which are well-marked, and perhaps a glint in the sand will reveal a piece of eight or doubloon (note that modern-day pirates such as the author have been known to leave replica coins at the site to enhance the thrill of the young explorer who makes the trek). While en route towards the point, keep a look out for the blue crab and manta rays that appear in the clear waters that surround the island. You don't need a glass bottom boat to see them, although finding the *Adventure* may be slightly more difficult. People consider it to perhaps be Blackbeard's "sugar ship", and pirate treasure may well have been buried with it under the ocean floor. Good luck.

The flagship of the pirate, the forty-cannon *Queen Anne's Revenge,* was run aground at Beaufort Inlet, then known as the *Sea of Caroline,* prior to the Battle of Ocracoke. Theories suggest that many of his crew were then marooned on the islands of the Inlet. Blackbeard had been a supporter of the Jacobite Revolution in England against King George ascending the throne, and thus named the ship as an act of protest and defiance. Located by marine archaeologists in 1996, relics from the ship are displayed at the Maritime Museum in Beaufort, a short jaunt on Highway 70 across the bridge from Morehead City. The museum is a must see for any would-be mariner or history buff, and a great spot to begin or conclude your paddle from Front Street.

Pioneer Paddles of the Colonial South

Beaufort, originally known as *Fish Towne,* is North Carolina's third oldest town, having been incorporated in 1722. It is home to the Rachel Carson Estuary (named for the author of the environmental classic, *Silent Spring*), a component of the North Carolina National Estuarine Research Reserve, which can be seen from the docks. Among the many houses that date back to the early 1700s is the Hammock House, circa 1709, which claims Blackbeard as being one of several sea captains that used the residence for occasional accommodations. The notorious buccaneer allegedly was angered by his 18 year-old French common-law wife while living at the home and hung her by the neck on an oak tree in the backyard. Legend or fact? No one can say for sure, but historians doubt the tale. The house is privately owned, but is only a short walk from the visitor center and can be viewed from street level. Union officers were quartered there during the Civil War. Another must see is the old burying ground, which includes the grave of a young girl who died at sea and was buried in a rum keg.

Take your pick among launch sites such as Perry Park or Fisherman's Park along Front Street, or the N.C. Wildlife Access, all which lead to a short crossing of Taylor's Creek to Carrot Island. Keep going and you will soon encounter numerous uninhabited beaches and an environment that resembles what the Carolina coast must have looked like hundreds of years before. Beaufort has little competition when it comes to island hopping capabilities. Carrot Island is adjacent to Shackleford Banks and home to a herd of what are thought to be Spanish Mustangs that have roamed wild for centuries. The Carson reserve includes 2,675 acres suitable for hiking, shelling, or simply exploring the natural salt flats and eelgrass beds. Only accessible by boat, the area features more than 200 species of birds at various times throughout the year. It is hard to imagine a more convenient colonial-style wilderness experience via paddle.

Spanish Mustangs roam Carrot Island in the Estuary

Beach your vessel for a picnic lunch or bottle of wine and then wander through the maritime forest on a treasure hunt to seek relics from a marooned buccaneer. If you choose a longer trek, the Cape Lookout National Seashore beckons on the opposite side of the estuary. Turn your compass north and take a few hours or a few days, as the seashore encompasses 56 miles of unspoiled barrier islands. You may not find a cache of doubloons, but testaments to the past abound from shark teeth to encapsulated ship relics. The latter was discovered by our son Dylan on a 2004 voyage to an unnamed island, and most certainly belonged to some pirate captain back in the day. Okay, well maybe. Do be cognizant of the weather and tidal flow, and

Pioneer Paddles of the Colonial South

take the fishing rods.

Turn the compass to the south and you will see Fort Macon State Park on the eastern end of Bogue Banks. The fort, active through World War II, is remarkably well-preserved and dates back to 1756. Civil War buffs probably know that the Confederate Army seized the fort in 1861, only to see it recaptured during General John Parke's campaign *(see the Hoophole Creek commentary later in this section)*. Town Creek Water Access is just across the bay, but be wary of commercial and motor boat traffic that can leave a wake high enough to swamp a canoe.

A trip to Beaufort would not be complete without a visit "Down East" along our Crystal Coast. Contrary to the uninformed popular belief, US 70 continues for miles into the easternmost part of the Cape Lookout National Seashore. Core Sound offers many access points that beckon to the paddler in areas such as Harkers Island, Sealevel and Drum Inlet. The Cedar Island National Wildlife Refuge is arguably the highlight of the region and you can launch on the creek just next to the ferry. Just follow US highway 70 until it ends, and then NC 12 until your road turns into waterway. From the island the Pamlico Sound resembles a calm ocean, with incredible sunsets that seem to naturally enhance when viewed from your kayak. Other than a few beach houses, particularly on the north end, one might think that time has stood still for centuries. Hopefully this area will escape the commercial homogenization that has beset so many areas of our Atlantic coastal paradise.

Before you leave the vicinity, be sure to visit Atlantic

William D. Auman

Beach and canoe or kayak across Bogue Sound on the south side of the Highrise Bridge. Next to the Atlantic Station shopping center off of Fort Macon Road, you will find a historical marker that pays tribute to Giovannie de Verrazano. Long before the days of Blackbeard, Verrazano was hired by King Francis I of France to explore the coast from Canada to Florida. He found a string of islands that he named Arcadia, meaning "for the beauty of the trees." The explorer thought he was in Asia when he was actually between Cape Fear and Cape Lookout, thought to be present-day Atlantic Beach and Morehead City. He described the area as having beautiful fields and broad plains, covered with immense forests various in color, too delightful and charming to be described.

The Atlantic Beach area of Bogue Sound also played host to a crossing of the Union Army on March 29, 1862, as forces under General John G. Parke came ashore at what is now known as Hoophole Creek. The Clean Water Management Fund has funded the preservation of this area as a Coastal Nature Preserve, and a trail to the sound is suitable for a short portage of your kayak. You can find the trailhead just next to the Coral Bay shopping center, marked by a Civil War Trails display. Don't forget to look for civil war musket balls along the shore among the scattering hermit crabs.

Continue South along NC 58 towards Emerald Isle and Swansboro and more opportunities to dip the paddle can easily be found. This area, akin to Beaufort yet on the southern tip of the Crystal Coast, hints of a bygone era when life was simple. The salty tang in the air still summons paddlers to the White Oak River, just as it did when privateer Captain Otway Burns was

Pioneer Paddles of the Colonial South

serving colonial America during the War of 1812. The grave of Captain Burns rests in Beaufort and his statute in the mountains of his namesake Burnsville, but he was a native son of what was then known as Swannsborough. This charming coastal village was built on the site of what was formerly an Algonquian town. The Algonquian tribe, also known as First Nation peoples, eventually made their way to Canada where a magical provincial park famous for its paddling trails now bears their name. You can access the White Oak River at Cedar Point and paddle upstream along the salt marsh until you reach the canals along the Tideland Trail.

     Before you depart, don't forget Hammocks Beach State Park with ferry service from Swansboro if you wish to kayak or canoe alongside more of North Carolina's beautiful unspoiled beaches. Getting to Bear Island, a gem of the park, can only be done by boat and is roughly a 2.5 mile paddle across Cow Channel if you forgo the ferry. The Tuscarora, later removed to New York where they became part of the Iroquois Confederacy, used Bear Island as a refuge during the 1711 and 1713 wars during which they unsuccessfully attempted to return encroaching colonists to their northern European homelands. Use the park's kayak launch and visit Huggins Island as well, which is adjacent to Bear and was home to a Confederate fort that burned in 1862, although earthworks remain. Queens Creek, where Captain Burns' homeplace once stood, can also be paddled either upstream from the park or downstream to the park from the Queen's Creek Road bridge. Just across the bridge from Swansboro is Cedar Point Access, another option for a paddle to Huggins Island or an even shorter trek across Hawkins Bay to Shark Tooth Island.

William D. Auman

Most of you probably know the difference between men such as Captain Burns, a privateer, and Captain Teach, a pirate (at least for the most part). Privateers were commissioned on behalf of their local governing body to attack foreign ships, while pirates would pillage and plunder for the benefit of themselves and their crew. The Carolina coast saw many of each breed. Many names of destinations within the Outer Banks hearken back to the pirate era. For example, Kill Devil Hills was allegedly christened as such due to the rum that would wash ashore after shipwrecks, which was foul enough to "kill the devil." In addition, Nags Head was a moniker derived from a pirate's ruse of tying a lantern to a horse to lure unsuspecting ships ashore.

Blackbeard, ever the illustrious buccaneer, traversed throughout the Eastern Seaboard from Pennsylvania to the Caribbean, but North Carolina holds the distinction of being home to his only "permanent" residence . That would be historic Bath, which later became our first incorporated town in 1705. Perhaps we should visit there prior to resuming our coastal exploration.

Historic Bath can be found east of "Little" Washington off of NC 92, approximately 45 miles inland just off the Pamlico River. A visitor's center is staffed full of friendly locals who will be happy to assist you. Don't miss St. Thomas Episcopal Church on Craven Street, the oldest European place of worship in the state, dating back to 1734. Also drop by the Palmer-Marsh House on Main Street which dates to 1751 and entertained the likes of the Marquis de Lafayette, among other notables.

Pioneer Paddles of the Colonial South

As for Blackbeard, the legendary pirate actually attempted to become a law-abiding citizen while a resident of the town, although he was ultimately lured back to the sea. If you paddle to Plum Point at the junction of Bath Creek and the Pamlico, you can see what are believed to be the foundational remains of the home that he and his fourteenth wife, sixteen year-old Mary Ormond, shared across the creek from their neighbor, Governor Charles Eden, who officiated at their nuptials. The *Ormand* surname is thought in genealogical circles to be a derivative of that of the author's original *Aumann,* so I have always claimed Blackbeard as an ancestral uncle. My father, a Navy veteran, is quick to disavow that suggestion! Plum Point is clearly visible from the waterfront, an area locally known as Bonner Point, and can be accessed by canoe in less than an hour. Many have searched for pirate booty at the site, but none has yet to be found.

History abounds at Bonner Point as well, which is where East Carolina University students have conducted extensive archaeological excavations. This is the locale where the legendary John Lawson chose to build his home, circa 1706. John's claim to fame may be as surveyor-general, but he also holds title as being the author of *A New Voyage to Carolina,* first published in 1709 and later appearing as *The History of Carolina.* But before Lawson, there were pirates in the vicinity.

Governor Eden, who some have accused of being in "cahoots" with his neighbor Blackbeard, had granted the pirate a King's pardon less than a month after Capt. Teach had conducted his highly profitable blockade of Charleston *(aka Charles Town until 1783, see the ensuing chapter).* Some say that Blackbeard

William D. Auman

had brought upwards of 1500 pounds of sterling with him to Bath Town, and many have been digging and metal detecting the snake and mosquito infested areas surrounding the creek for years. Bath Creek runs right alongside Main and is only a short paddle from its confluence with the Pamlico. When he left Bath to return to pirating, legend has it that Blackbeard cursed the town, forbidding it from growing any larger than it was during his time there. 17th century Bath boasted a population of some 8,000 people, but today less than 300 residents call it home, so do we have impact from the supernatural or a continuum of dark magic?

If you make your way to Bath, don't neglect to paddle Goose Creek. The state park lies only a few miles west on NC highway 92, with an entrance just off state road 1334. There is a developed camping area that sits creek side with numerous points from which to launch your canoe or kayak. Head south and you will soon reach the Pamlico just after Flatty Creek appears on your left, another must-see segment of your paddling expedition. Be wary of the many Osprey nests that predominate among the Bald Cypress or you could be dive bombed by an angry raptor. A pleasant afternoon can be spent simply floating along and watching those intriguing fish hawks catch their evening meal with their talons. Fishing in the brackish water is excellent as well and a variety of species, from Redfish to Largemouth Bass, can readily be caught.

If you are fortunate enough to bring along a preschool paddler, continue on to Washington and visit the North Carolina Estaurarium on the banks of the Pamlico River. The intricate world of the marine biologist awaits the young explorer, and you can always drop your canoe from the dock and paddle downstream into the estuary. Although slightly influenced by the tide, this segment of the Pamlico offers flatwater with little current for an easy out-and-back trek.

More coastal area paddling sites abound in this wonderfully undeveloped section of the state, including historic Edenton which features its own colonial park adjacent to the bay. Launch at the park and paddle east under the bridge on Queen Anne's Creek or west toward Pembroke Creek. In October, 1774, 51 women from Edenton signed a statement affirming support for the first North Carolina Provincial Congress' decision to boycott British goods in the colonies. This protest, one of the earliest that was written and organized by American women, became known as the Edenton Tea Party.

North of Edenton we find the Perquimans River, wherein lies Durant's Neck just southeast of Hertford. I include this because recorded in the Perquiman's County Registrar's office we find the deed associated with the first land transaction in North Carolina between a white man (George Durant) and an Indian Chief known as Kilcocanen, which is dated March 1, 1661. Kilcocanen was associated with the Yeopim tribe along the river whose name is translated as the "Land of Beautiful Women" and flows into the tidal estuary known as Albemarle Sound. Given that Indigenous Peoples generally considered themselves as caretakers of their lands as opposed to owners, it would be interesting to know more about the context within which this "sale" occurred. As for Durant, records show him to have been a leader in Culpeper's Rebellion of 1677-78, a precursor to the subsequent American Revolution, which saw colonists rebel against the Lords Proprietors due to a variety of complaints, including an English tax on tobacco. *Author's note: The Lords Proprietors were the eight Englishmen to whom King Charles, in 1663 and 1665, granted joint ownership of a tract of land in the New World to be known as "Carolina."*

There are several access points in the area, including the boat ramp on Granby Street in Hertford, Punch Road just upstream, Mill Creek on the north side of the river, Goodwin Creek to the west and Sutton Creek to the east. There are over 40 miles of paddling trails in the vicinity, so do your homework and pick your best option.

Pioneer paddles continue along the southern coast, also known as the Cape Fear region, where we also find a fair share of additional pirate history. Many believe that the infamous Captain William Kidd buried his ill-gotten booty on Gardiners Island off Long Island, New York, but oral tradition offers a differing account. Kidd was accused of piracy in 1698 when he captured a French ship heavily laden with gold, silver and jewels. As a privateer, this would normally have been acceptable, yet the French ship was captained by an Englishman. Kidd began to sail north towards his New York home with a plan to bury the treasure, which would enable him to recover the same if he were to be later exonerated. In 1699, he passed the beautiful and uninhabited land of Greenville Sound, near present-day Wrightsville Beach, and purportedly chose a scenic island full of oak and yaupon to bury his loot in two iron chests. He then paid a shipmate, John Redfield, to live across from the island and guard the treasure until his return.

Pioneer Paddles of the Colonial South

Kidd never returned and was publicly hanged in London in 1701. Redfield subsequently moved to Charleston, South Carolina, where he enjoyed the spoils of his guardianship, but one of his descendants later returned to the island and supposedly discovered one of the chests. My friend Kyle and I recently attempted to dig for the other, but we only had plastic spoons to use and were thus unsuccessful. For an easy out-and-back treasure hunt, put in next to the bridge on Bradley Creek and paddle southeast with right turn into what is now the Intracoastal Waterway (ICW). Soon the still uninhabited "Money Island" will appear in the middle of the sound. Don't forget the metal detector and shovel!

Dominated by the historic port city of Wilmington, days could be spent touring what has become North Carolina's most populous coastal region. You are, however, only about an hour or so from the Grand Strand and Myrtle Beach, so watch out for the company of power boats and spring breakers on jet skis. No offense, but some of those characters seem to enjoy annoying even the most tolerant of paddlers. The majority, however, will properly cut their engine to minimize wake. Be sure to hit waves at an angle so as to limit the chance of a swell sending you into an unexpected swim.

Paddle along the Cape Fear's wharf area in Wilmington and you will find many restored 18th century homes, together with the World War II battleship *North Carolina,* who participated in every major offensive naval battle in the Pacific Theater and earned 15 battle stars. While gawking at the 728 foot ship, be sure to stay close to shore and avoid the wake from the omnipresent commercial vessels. You may not find the same degree of wilderness that points further north or south may offer, but the occasional shallow inlet that only the paddler can access will lead to a nice respite for a picnic or beverage break.

Just north of the Wilmington area lies Topsail Island, a relic of coastal preservation unto itself. Topsail is family friendly, 26 miles from north to south, and offers generally calm waterways from which you can explore the inlet. Much of Topsail remains as it was from the days of my childhood and it is easy to find many paddle "put in" sites along the sound side road. It is a short venture across open water to enter a realm of wilderness, home to the blue crabs, clams and oysters that predominate the habitat. The salt marsh serves as a natural barrier between the sound and the ICW, creating an atmosphere that should remain free of commercial interference.

Further north along NC 50 you will find Surf City, known more for its saltwater fishing reputation as opposed to the Beach Boys or Jan and Dean surfing crowd. Keep going straight on NC 210, pass through North Topsail, and you will soon cross the ICW. Drop your paddle at the public access area on the inland side of the bridge. From there you can paddle north among the marsh to Alligator Bay or south towards Goose Bay. Salt marsh wilderness is abundant in both directions of this area that is among the least developed within the Cape Fear region.

Back in 1728 a guy named Emmett established a ferry near Pollock's Point on the New River just across the bay, which was followed in 1759 by a companion ferry operated by Robert Snead. Snead left a bigger footprint since his ferry, which was a key element for trade on the post road linking Virginia to

Pioneer Paddles of the Colonial South

Charleston, South Carolina, later became the namesake for the village of Snead's Ferry. My local friend Kevin and I enjoy putting in at the point and paddling across Snead's Creek in order to quietly and tactfully invade the marine base known as Camp Lejeune, which offers a nice sandbar with no signage to discourage entry. If one subsequently appears, think back to the advice of Woody Guthrie (also mentioned in the preceding chapter) who proclaimed in his folk classic *This Land in Your Land*, that the other side of the sign with nothing on it was made for you and me! You may need to make a quick exit, just look out for submarines if you are discovered.

  Masonboro Inlet Coastal Reserve and The Point on Oak Island are both favorited area options further south. The former can be accessed at Trails End Park, with a chain of uninhabited barrier islands ripe for exploration within reach after a short paddle across the inlet. The latter is a spot popular with locals, but allows for an inland paddle along the Lockwood Folly River that can lead to private beach areas on Horse Island. Sheep Island is just across from the launch and offers hiking and fishing opportunities.

  Further south we find Zeke's Island National Estaurine Research Reserve just past Fort Fisher. During the Civil War, Fort Fisher kept Wilmington's port open to blockade-runners that supplied necessary goods to the Confederate armies inland. It ultimately became the last remaining supply route for Generals Robert E. Lee and Joseph E. Johnston, but fell to the Union after a massive amphibious assault on January 15, 1865, leading to an end to one of the most destructive and divisive conflicts that our nation has ever endured.

William D. Auman

Returning to the present, I highly recommend the Zeke's Island paddle which has easy access at Federal Point, adjacent to the Southport Ferry landing into the Basin. Paddle north and remaining earthworks from the fort are visible, but turn towards the east and paddle parallel to the Rock, a low rock wall built well over a hundred years ago, and you will reach the island after about a mile. Take a break on the beach to explore the maritime forest complete with windswept oak trees and yucca plants, then continue to the backside of the island where a lagoon awaits. North Island and No-Name Island are also within the preserve and worthy of a stop as well if time, wind and tide allow.

Also in the vicinity we find Carolina Beach State Park, just off US 421 to the right as you approach the beach town's city limit. Home to the renowned cannibal of the horticultural world, the Venus Flytrap, the park offers the opportunity to hike through a maritime forest and see the Flytrap in its natural element. Given that the species grows wild only in bogs and savannahs within a 100 mile radius of Wilmington, you can take advantage of what most only view when visiting their local exotic plant nursery. While there, be sure to paddle Snows Cut, which meanders through the park from the intracoastal to Myrtle Grove Sound.

A final coastal jaunt can time-travel you back to May of 1664, when John Vassall sailed to Carolina from Barbados and chose a settlement site for the original Charles Towne on a high bluff on the west side of the Cape Fear River, north of Town Creek in what is now Brunswick County. A fortified compound was erected and within two years about 800 people had settled in the colony, but indigenous peoples did not appreciate the encroachment and were hostile to the newcomers. In addition, pirates interfered with supply efforts and the colony was abandoned in 1667 in favor of developing a second Charles Towne backed by many of the same Barbadians. This was accomplished in 1670 on the Ashley River in what later developed into the modern-day port city of Charleston, South Carolina. More on that to come.

Although there is a public kayak launch on Town Creek bordering Brunswick Forest, a shorter trek to the 1664 site can begin at the Gator Hole, a country store that sits on the creek just off of NC 133. From there you only have about 2 miles to where the creek empties into the Cape Fear, with the old settlement slightly upstream to the north. There are ample places to beach your vessel and explore, but hopefully you will be more successful than I in that I have yet to discover any signs of the 350+ year-old compound. The area is, however, still undeveloped and lends to a communal spirit with those brave souls who attempted to carve a new life out of the maritime forests in the region so many years ago.

There are important lessons to be learned from a family paddling excursion to the site, which showed the "Gator Hole" to have been aptly named. Although North Carolina is the northernmost state that is home to the alligator, I didn't expect to count eleven of them sunning themselves along the creek bank during an April paddle. Had I been more prepared, I would have left our canine companion "Rasta" at home, since she tried to jump off our canoe after every one and had to be leashed to the thwart for her own safety. I would also advise you to not only time your trip to coincide with tidal flow, but also consider any predicted wind pattern changes. When you fail to do the latter, you could subject yourselves to headwinds that are stronger than the tidal influence and can create a situation that is far from the marital bliss that normally accompanies our paddling experiences.

Searching for the original Charles Towne with Rasta

Moving on, many of you are no doubt aware that North Carolina is divided into three somewhat distinct regions: the coastal plain, piedmont and mountains. "From the mountains to the sea" is a familiar descriptive refrain for our state, but for paddling purposes I am deviating somewhat and moving gradually inland from the coast to the coastal plain to highlight more of what our eastern seaboard offers the pioneer paddler.

Pioneer Paddles of the Colonial South

Section Three: Revolutionary Patriots among Ancient Forests

Journey with me back to February 27, 1776 and paddle into the history of the Battle of Moore's Creek Bridge. Follow Highway 421 about 20 miles northwest from Wilmington, then go west on NC 210 for 5 miles into the National Park. Put in off the park road near the picnic area and listen closely for the ghostly sounds of the fife and drum core as they echo through the forest, which remains relatively undeveloped in this remote region dominated by farmland. It is a short paddle to the reconstructed bridge, where a group of approximately 150 Patriots under Colonels Alexander Lillington and Richard Caswell defeated a larger force of Loyalists in a battle that effectively ended royal authority in the eastern section of the colony. The creek, a tributary of the Black River, winds through swampy terrain which at the time could only be crossed by use of the bridge. Lillington's troops arrived at the bridge a day ahead of the Loyalists and prepared earthworks on the high ground across from the bridge, the remnants of which can be still be seen today. When the Loyalists attacked, their broadswords were met with a barrage of musket and artillery fire, leaving some 30 dead. The Patriots suffered only one casualty, and locals say that his apparition can still be seen haunting the swamp during a full moon.

After the Patriot victory at Moore's Creek, the Fourth North Carolina Provincial Congress met in Halifax. On April 12, 1776, members unanimously adopted the Halifax Resolves,

William D. Auman

which ordered the North Carolina delegation in Philadelphia to seek and vote for independence. This action made our state the first of the colonial governments to call for independence and the signing date of the instrument remains today as one of two that appears on the North Carolina flag and seal. The other date that appears would be May 20, 1775, when the Mecklenburg Declaration of Independence was promulgated in Charlotte. Drafted a full year before Thomas Jefferson penned the national declaration, four copies were delivered by Captain James Jack on a daring horseback ride to the Second Continental Congress in Philadelphia. Books have been written with evidence to corroborate the premise that Jefferson had in fact plagiarized certain segments of his account. More on that later.

Just up the road from Moore's Creek paddlers will find the Northeast Cape Fear River in Pender County. Take exit 398 off of Interstate 40, then NC 53 East to County Road 1512, which dead ends at the access point. Take a right around the bend at the put-in and venture upstream to Holly Shelter Creek, which enters on the left after about a half mile. If you continue up the main channel of the Northeast Cape, the mouth of Ashes Creek will soon appear on your left. Both Holly Shelter and Ashes allow for an optional course of exploration, and each offers side channels in both directions that only a canoe or kayak can navigate. This area offers terrific solitude and only a negligble amount of motorboat traffic, but be wary of area hunters if in season.

The water clarity that you will encounter is a mystical dark tea color, owing to the tannic acid that permeates most rivers and creeks in North Carolina's coastal plain. Thanks to the juniper, gum, and cypress trees robust with Spanish moss, bacteria cannot grow in the water, so I never hesitate to dive in for a swim should the opportunity present. Before the days of refrigeration, the water was thought to be chemically pure and if regularly drunk would promote long life. Perhaps Ponce de Leon should have been searching for his fountain of youth in eastern North Carolina?

Not far from Wilmington lies the 2,757 acre hammock of Roan Island, which adjoins abandoned rice fields in an area flanked by both the Cape Fear and Black Rivers. Thanks to the Nature Conservancy, a large majority of the island will live forever in a blissful state of coastal wilderness. Only a boat will get you there, as no bridge connects directly to the island. From US 421, turn left on NC 210 and head west past Moore's Creek. After crossing the Black River, take a left on Canetuck Road (SR 1104) and then a quick left on Heading Bluff Road (SR 1103). Small boat access can be found at the Lyon's Creek bridge in about 2 miles. Paddle southeast and the island will soon appear. Turn right and the creek will merge into the Cape Fear, or take a left and you will soon be paddling the Black. A former logging area, the isolated Roan is now home to black bear, deer, bobcat, alligator, and incredible fishing. Keep in mind that rivers do remain tidal in this vicinity as well.

For the ultimate time-travel experience, let's move the colonial-era clock back to a time estimated to be 605 years before Jesus Christ was born. I couldn't make this up if I tried. Within the Three Sisters Swamp off of the Black River lies a bald cypress tree known as BLK 227, whose core samples have been radiocarbon dated to reveal an age of 2,629 years. Thanks to the team lead by Professor David Stahle of the University of Arkansas, we now know that numerous trees in the swamp have reached 1,000+ years, making them the oldest living organisms ever to be found in North America east of California.

A word of warning...if you choose to paddle within the Three Sisters Swamp, please utilize a local guide as it is easy to get lost amidst the local water moccasins and friendly mosquitoes that love to prey on paddling visitors. The Black River Preserve features over 17,000 acres of protected land along the water, so other options for exploration are abundant. Wildlife Resource Commission access points lie at Ivanhoe north of the swamp and at Hunts Bluff just south, or you could opt to put in at Newby's Landing for a nominal sum and paddle upstream about two miles to the edge of the swamp. Many ancient cypress with trunks large enough to drive a car through can be found in this area as well. Henry's Landing is another private launch just downstream from Ivanhoe and about five miles north of the swamp.

More ancient trees lie further north within the coastal plain. Perhaps my favorite paddle within the region features a forest befitting the wizards and druids from whence its name is evoked: The "Enchanted Forest" of Merchants Millpond StatePark. Directions to the forest are whimsical—take the canoe trail to the campsites, the follow the yellow buoys through the millpond, turn right at the last island, bear left at the beaver

Pioneer Paddles of the Colonial South

The author with paddling partner Trouble on the edge of Three-Sisters Swamp shadowed by an ancient Bald Cypress

lodge, paddle along the shoreline, find a channel into Lassiter Swamp, then head straight until morning. Even in the light of day the forest stirs primordial instinct and casts a spell, but in reality the paddle is only about 2 miles from the millpond put in. Trees have never been cut in this ancient grove, where 1,000+ year-old bald cypress mingle with tupelo gums with Spanish moss draping their canopy.

Often described as being a cross between Florida's Everglades and Georgia's Okefenokee, the centerpiece of the park is the pond itself, which was formed in 1811 when Bennett's Creek was dammed to power a gristmill. At only 3,250 acres, the relatively small park is home to one of the most diverse collections of plant and animal life in the mid-Atlantic, from beaver to bear to the poisonous cottonmouth. Over 200 varieties of birds and mammals, together with approximately 70 species of amphibians and reptiles and 150 assorted water plants watch as visiting paddlers join their ecological wonderland.

Merchants Millpond is easy to reach from US 158 and lies between the communities of Gatesville and Sunbury. It is approximately 30 miles from the towns of Ahoskie, Elizabeth City, and Edenton. A family canoe-in campground is available for an overnight stay, and don't be surprised if inquisitive otters play hide and seek with your crew as you paddle in. Primitive camping is also available, and canoes may be rented if necessary. Family-friendly hiking trails surround the pond if you wish to beach the boat and enjoy a diversionary land excursion.

Fast-forwarding in reverse to the colonial era, an excellent pioneer paddle can be found at the Snow Hill access for Contentnea Creek, a tributary of the Neuse River, in Greene County. Easy flat-water paddling with more big cypress trees awaits in either an up or downstream direction. Nearby, along a stream known as Fort Run, was the site of Neoheroka Fort. Neoheroka was considered to be the last stronghold of the Tuscarora, many of whom, as previously noted, ultimately fled to New York to become part of the Iroquois Confederacy. On March 23, 1713, colonial militiamen killed or captured approximately 950 Indians in a battle along the creek, marking a tragic end to the resistance of the Tuscarora and their coastal Algonkian allies in North Carolina.

The conflict had begun back in 1711 as encroaching Europeans continued to claim more land from the Native Americans in an effort to support their growing colony. The

Pioneer Paddles of the Colonial South

Tuscarora at first would appear as friendly visitors to the settlers' farms and later strike suddenly from ambush. The colony of North Carolina did not have enough manpower or money to defeat the tribe, but help came from neighboring South Carolina, which took the opportunity to enrich itself by ultimately looting Tuscarora towns and taking slaves. Many were later sold to waiting South Carolina traders in exchange for guns and merchandise—a sad footnote to the colonists victory.

Pioneer patriarch John Lawson is also infamously connected to this area, having met an untimely death at the hands of the Tuscarora during a canoe voyage back in September of 1711 along the Neuse River. Lawson, together with associate Christopher von Graffenreid, were captured and taken as hostages to the town of Catechna (near modern day Snow Hill). Graffenreid had been instrumental in transporting groups of German and Swiss refugees to lands along the Neuse near what is now New Bern. After insulting, rather than placating their captors, both were tortured and killed.

Yet another major conflict on the soil of Carolina also predated the American Revolution, that being the Regulator Rebellion, which could be categorized as a precursor that helped light the flame of revolt. Many settlers in the western coastal plain and eastern piedmont were becoming increasingly disgruntled with the provincial government's excessive taxes, illegal fees and localized political corruption, choosing to form an association of "Regulators" in 1768. After peaceful negotiations failed, the Regulators began to disrupt court proceedings, refused to pay tariffs and fees, and terrorized those who administered the law.

William D. Auman

On May 16, 1771, Governor William Tryon marched west from the colonial capitol of New Bern with an army of approximately 1,000 men to the banks of Great Alamance Creek in the heart of Regulator country, where about 2,000 dissenters, largely farmers, awaited him. He gave the Regulators a choice—to return peacefully to their homes or be fired upon. "Fire and be damned!" was their unfortunate answer, as they were soon crushed by the governor's army. The battle was recently depicted in the television series *Outlander.* Alamance County is home to the historical battle site along the creek, although water levels are generally too low to paddle the roughly four miles upstream from the public access area on Main Street in Graham. I came close, but then opted for the downstream trek to the mouth of the creek, which ultimately leads to Swepsonville River Park on the Haw River. I would encourage you inspiring regulators to consult the Haw River Paddle Trail online, which includes fourteen potential access sites in Alamance County.

As for New Bern, from whence Governor Tryon came before he abdicated North Carolina to take the "throne" of New York, I suggest a put-in on the Trent River at Pollocksville for a wilderness trek through the Croaton National Forest. Although you could continue downstream all the way past the refurbished Tryon Palace in New Bern, a quieter option would be to venture upstream on Mill Creek which appears about a half-mile southeast from the launch. The national forest features 160,000 acres of pine forest, bogs, raised swamps known as pocosins, and eventually saltwater estuaries. Bordered on three sides by tidal rivers such as the Trent and Bogue Sound at the coast, the forest is truly defined by water. Longleaf pine savannas once dominated the southeastern coastal plain, but 98 percent of them are gone due to logging and the emerging dominance of other species. The Croatan harbors some remaining strands from the colonial era (up to 300 years old), and in 2002 the Forest Service embarked upon a plan that calls for restoration of the landscape to pre-European settlement conditions! A great idea, but no need to wait for the complete transformation, as the national forest offers unique paddling opportunities every day of the year right now.

Lake paddlers can choose from Catfish Lake (access off of FR 158), Great Lake (off FR 126), or the adjoining Long, Little and Ellis Lakes. All are approximately 10 miles west of Havelock as the crow flies. Public boat ramps also provide access to the Neuse and White Oak Rivers, in addition to Cahooque and Brice Creeks. The latter is a favorite pilgrimage, beginning in the Sheep Ridge Wilderness and following north to its juncture with the Trent River just south of New Bern. A popular put-in is the Wildlife Resource Commission access on FR 121-A, which offers a downstream paddle of approximately 2.5 miles to the Trent. For more seclusion, try the Lee's Bridge crossing off of FR 111.

We can't leave the coastal plain without exploring our unique bay lakes with their imaginative origin stories, which range from alien meteorites crashing into the earth to dinosaurs creating sinkholes that ultimately filled with water. Waccamaw Siouans still today refer to themselves as "People of the Falling Star," referencing the meteor that fell from the night sky leaving a crater that filled with water, creating a lake now known as Waccamaw. The accepted scientific truth, however, is as follows: as glaciers waxed and waned in regions north of us, water-filled depressions expanded and contracted from wind and wave patterns, forming sand deposits around the waters edge.

Let's begin with Lake Waccamaw, a timeless treasure that tourists seem to whiz by while in a hurry to get to the Cape Fear beaches, although it is only a short detour off of US 74. A five-mile trail runs along the south side of the lake, which encompasses approximately 9,000 acres of remarkably shallow water with an average depth of only seven feet. Home to 52 different species of fish, some of which are found nowhere else in the world, this natural wonder has the distinction of being home to the largest variety of finned creatures within the Old North State.

Fish aren't the only native inhabitants, however, that are predominant at Lake Waccamaw. Be wary of the omnipresent alligator and water moccasin. A sizable population of each call the area home, but most are relatively harmless if left alone. A direct descendant of the dinosaur, our Carolina gators first appeared over 250 million years ago. Keep in mind that they can outrun a human for about the equivalent of a 40-yard dash, so be sure to observe them from a safe distance.

To explore the lake, try putting in at the state park which is located at the end of the road on the northeast shoreline among the limestone bluffs that rise from the swampy terrain. Canoe camping works well at the park, which requires a short portage of gear from the parking area to the camp sites. Paddlers can also access the lake at the Columbus County Access Area near the visitor center, or the Wildlife Resources Commission ramp on the west side. Be prepared to share the immediate vicinity of

Pioneer Paddles of the Colonial South

these latter choices with a motorboat or two. As an alternative, drive to the end of Waccamaw Shores Road and you will reach the spillway, which is otherwise known as the headwaters of the Waccamaw River. This is a great spot to launch from if you tire of exploring the grass beds, cypress, and lily pads that lie along the edge of the lakeshore. The swampy river snakes its way (or should I say "moccasins" its way due to the prevalence of that deadly reptile) all the way to the Atlantic, where it enters not far from the Grand Strand in South Carolina. It is a perfect setting for an "out and back" day trip due to the slow current and lack of tidal influence at this point inland, but bring the mosquito repellent.

Some canoe buffs such as yours truly enjoy a historical quest to not only paddle into history, but also to nourish an inherent appreciation for the origins of the opportunity to do so. To that end, you may wish to visit the impressive display of wood/canvas and birchbark canoes that can be found at the Adirondack Museum in Blue Mountain, New York, or for that matter the Canadian Canoe Museum in Peterborough, Ontario. The Golden Lake Algonquin First Nation Community in Ontario likewise exhibits traditional birchbark paddle craft, some of which date back to the 1850s. But for those of you who would rather not venture so far from home, a significant portion of such history can be found in our own backyard.

The Objibway, Huron, Micmac, and other northeastern tribes may lay claim to the remarkable invention of the birchbark canoe, just as the French fur traders bear responsibility for its adaption from a bark base to that of wood/canvas. However, long before either invention, in coastal Carolina the Tuscarora,

William D. Auman

Croatan, and others burned and scraped giant cypress and pine into dugout canoes. Heavy but functional, the dugouts were used for hunting, fishing, and basic transportation through our swamps and rivers. A trio of teenagers actually discovered a 940 year-old pine dugout in Lake Waccamaw in 2021 while swimming in the lake!

At Pettigrew State Park, seven miles south of Creswell off of US 64, we find North Carolina's second largest natural lake and an impressive number of ancient dugouts. Lake Phelps lies off a vast peninsula between the Albemarle Sound and Pamlico River, and is thought to be over 38,000 years old. Although archaeologists have uncovered thousands of pottery fragments and projectile points, the most fascinating discovery is a collection of over 30 dugout canoes which are believed to have been sunk by seasonal native American hunters in the lake's shallow water. One of the canoes is 37 feet in length, the longest known dugout to exist in the southeast. Another has been carbon dated to be 4,380 years old. With the exception of a few at the visitor center and one at the Museum of History in Raleigh, the canoes remain in the lake which serves to protect against their dissipation.

Lake Phelps boasts over 16,600 acres of water to explore. Several man-made canals enter on the north/northeast shore, and it is generally easy to find a spot to launch for paddling. A boat ramp can be found near Somerset Place, a state historic site and plantation from the antebellum south. Civil War buffs can visit the grave of Confederate General James Johnston Pettigrew just off the old carriage road. Gen. Pettigrew, the park's namesake, led the North Carolina 26th regiment in the

Pioneer Paddles of the Colonial South

high-water mark charge at the Battle of Gettysburg. He died thereafter after being wounded during General Robert E. Lee's retreat following the battle.

Nestled amidst this "blackwater country," and rising from the wetlands of Lake Phelps, you will find the historical Scuppernong River. Meandering through some 26 miles of swamp forest, the river is thought to have begun some 4,000 years ago, increasing in size as the climate warmed. European farmers arrived in the 1600s, and African-American slaves eventually dug a canal connecting the lake to the river which offered agrarian products an outlet for export to the merchant sailors who waited downstream.

The Scuppernong is generally comfortable (temperature & mosquito-wise that is) year-round, and offers little to no current with an abundance of relatively undeveloped and remote inland wilderness. A favorite short trek is to put-in at Riders Creek off SR 1105 and paddle a little over 2 miles to the Columbia waterfront, which makes for an easy bicycle return shuttle. For a longer adventure, you can begin at either Spruill's Bridge off SR 1142 (15.5 miles to Columbia), or Cross Landing (9.5 miles to Columbia), all of which offer greenway paddling through a swamp forest of cypress, juniper and gum. A short distance from the river the forest gives way to pocosins, unique shrub bogs built upon layers of peat. The name ironically is one of several attributed to the Alonquians, and translates into *"swamp on a hill."*

The Mattamuskeet National Wildlife Refuge can be found a short crow's fly to the southeast of Pettigrew, and boasts

William D. Auman

a 40,000 acre centerpiece known as Lake Mattamuskeet. Indigenous Peoples hold claim to designating the lake to be known as *"Mata-mackya-t-wi"*, which means "moving swamp." Lake Mattamuskeet is a true paddlers dream, 18 miles long, 5 to 6 miles wide, and only averaging approximately 2 feet in depth. A former hunting ground of the Algonquians, the lake provides a valuable wintering refuge for thousands of snowbirds, including geese and tundra swans that travel along the Atlantic Flyway.

Drive east from Belhaven along US 264, or south from Columbia on highway 94, and the lake will seemingly appear out of nowhere. NC 94 divides the lake in half and offers boat access just before you reach the southern shoreline. Other access points abound along the lakeshore, just don't forget to bring the rod and reel for world-class largemouth bass angling. Deer, bobcat, otters, and the occasional black bear are among the 'critters that call the refuge home. Words cannot begin to describe the beauty of this remote, yet family-friendly wilderness.

Not far away yet another refuge beckons to the paddler. The Alligator River National Wildlife Refuge encompasses over 150,000 acres of wetland habitat that is home to a tremendous variety of wildlife species, ranging from the alligator to the relocated and thriving red wolf *(canis rufus)*, brought back from the brink of extinction no doubt to appease N.C. State Wolfpack fans such as the author! Keep north on NC Hwy 94 from Mattamuskeet and you will pass through the Pocosin Lakes National Wildlife Refuge while en route to Columbia. Take a right on US 64, head east and cross the Albemarle Sound. A right on Buffalo City Road will take you to the refuge headquarters. Milltail Creek traverses the heart of the seemingly road-less refugee, and you can paddle a variety of water trails ranging from about 1.5 to 5.5 miles. Sawyer Lake also can make for a nice day trip, but you may run into a motorboat or two, not to mention a hunting party if in season, so be sure to exercise due caution.

Further inland lies a favorite haunt of mine that is not found on many maps or guide books, but I'll risk local wrath by disclosing what is known as Rhodes Pond (after all, I live in the mountains or in Florida now anyway). About 15 miles north of Fayetteville, just off of US 301, sits Mingo Swamp, which can be accessed roadside, but pay attention or you'll zoom by and miss the put-in. Locals with their cane poles often line the shoreline and fish for bream (aka bluegill), catfish and "jack" (aka chain pickerel), but you will soon leave them behind as you venture into the blackwater swamp. No other roads or developed areas can be found along the shore, and towering bald cypress draped in Spanish moss rise from the waters of the pond. Rhodes Pond probably qualifies as a small lake as its size is comparable to others so designated within the region, such as Holts Lake and Quaker Neck Lake, yet provides an easily accessible wilderness experience. Embark at sunrise and paddle into another dimension with twilight zone aura as the fog rises off the water. Drift along on a sultry day and ride its sluggish waters filled with duckweed-- just remember that natural systems never make haste. There is a certain calm that attaches to the serenity of the setting.

Jones Lake State Park is a close neighbor to Rhodes and home to the bay lakes of Jones and Salters that lie within the

William D. Auman

Cape Fear basin. Take NC 53 south from Fayetteville, then left on NC 242 and the state park will appear in about a mile. The lakes are part of the state forest game land of 32,237 acres known as Bladen Lakes, and the adjacent area is swamp in all directions with primitive camping allowed. Salters Lake, which is named for American Revolutionary heroine Sallie Salters who would spy on Tories encamped nearby, requires four-wheel drive capability and a ranger to open the gate for access, whereas Jones features a kayak launch next to the parking area.

Lake Singletary, the deepest of the bay lakes with a maximum depth of about twelve feet, is another area cousin that also features a state park with access off of NC 53 approximately five miles south of the 242 turnoff. Settled by colonists under the leadership of Richard Singletary, who received a land grant in 1729 from the provincial government, it offers another taste of easily accessible colonial-style wilderness for the adventuring paddler.

Continuing to zigzag back and forth across the coastal plain, let's navigate our time machine back to the northeast and experience an area that time has truly forgotten—the Great Dismal Swamp. The father of our country, that same guy who chopped down the old Cherry Tree, was truly an ecologist at

Pioneer Paddles of the Colonial South

The author's restored wooden kayak at Salters Lake, built at Tooker's Boatyard, Long Island, NY, between 1900-1920 by Sam Newey

heart. George Washington himself described the Great Dismal Swamp in May of 1763 as "a glorious paradise...neither plain nor hollow, but a hillside." Washington orchestrated the surveying and digging of a 5-mile ditch from the western edge of the swamp to Lake Drummond, a lovely circular body of water that covers over 3,000 acres and lies just over the border in Virginia. The swamp itself originally spread over nearly 2200 square miles, but due to clearing and drainage for cultivation purposes, the current size stands at approximately 600 miles. It's simple to drop paddle in the canal at the Dismal Swamp Canal Visitor Center on US 17 in South Mills, which allows for a blackwater outing in either direction.

William D. Auman

A land of mystical folklore, the tale perhaps best known is the Lady of the Lake, canonized by Irish poet Thomas Moore in 1803. Locals say that an Indian maiden who died just before her wedding day is periodically seen paddling her ghostly white canoe across the waters of the swamp. Moore's poem, "The Lake of the Dismal Swamp," tells how her bereaved lover came to believe that his lost love had departed her grave and taken to the swamp. He followed her and never returned, reuniting with her as they continue to paddle as one spirit. Other ghosts abound, primarily due to the Civil War Battle of South Mills in 1862, which eventually enabled the Union to capture control of this important transportation route. Thereafter, a number of Confederate deserters hid out in the swamp and made occasional raids on federal boats. In December of 1863, General Edward A. Wild attempted to capture the rebels and in the process burned settlements, hung innocent men, and took women as hostages. Such action led Governor Zebulon B. Vance, a native of Weaverville, to refer to Wild as a "disgrace to the manhood of the age." Vance, himself a slave-holder, has a very mixed legacy within the annals of history that can be explored more thoroughly through a visit to his birthplace, a state historic site.

The swamp is replete with history, and mention must be made of its service as a natural refuge for runaway slaves. Following the American Revolution, many fleeing African-Americans chose to join a colony of "maroons" in the swamp, which was at the time such an inhospitable place that sanctuary came naturally. The actions of a few, however, who preyed on unwary swamp travelers, caused much alarm among residents living near the swamp. In 1831, a brutal slave uprising lead by Nat Turner resulted in the butchering of 55 men, women and children in a community known as Courtland, Virginia. Similar unrest had been reported in nearby Camden and Elizabeth City, North Carolina. A militia force, complete with dogs, was thereby sent to wipe out the runaway slave colonies, and many were killed. In 1842, Henry Wadsworth Longfellow memorialized this chapter in the swamp's dismal past with his poem, "The Slave in Dismal Swamp."

While in the area, journey east of Elizabeth City to an often overlooked blackwater stream known as Indiantown Creek. The Camden County Chamber of Commerce publishes a trail map that includes Indiantown, which covers some 30,000 acres of North River Game Land and is adjacent to our Wildlife Resource Commission's black bear sanctuary. Some of North Carolina's last remaining virgin bald cypress and Atlantic White Cedar can be visited in this primeval coastal wilderness, which represents an immediate escape from contemporary urban society. The trail begins as a drainage canal on SR 1148, but a public landing off Indiantown Road is more accessible. It is possible to continue downstream to the North River and take out at Coinjock along the Intracoastal Waterway, but that makes for a long day given a distance of approximately 15 miles or so. Accordingly, you may wish to plan for an out-and-back day trip. The trail is well marked thanks to its identification as part of the Albemarle Region Canoe and Small Boat Trails System.

Just north of Rocky Mount off of US 301, on the south bank of the Roanoke River, you will find more colonial history in the former port town of Halifax. North Carolina's Fourth Provincial Congress met here in the spring of 1776, and on April 12 delegates unanimously enacted the first legislation by an

William D. Auman

original colony that called for independence from England. Who knew at the time that within two months the entire nation would follow suit? Ironically, the first reading of the U.S. Declaration (again, arguably edited by Thomas Jefferson from the Mecklenburg Declaration of Independence of May 20, 1775) occurred at the Halifax Courthouse site on August 1, 1776. Public river access is no longer available in Halifax, but at the visitor center one of the volunteers, clad in 1700-era attire, can direct you to points upstream at Weldon or downstream near Scotland Neck. The Roanoke is known for some potential hazards so be sure to seek local advice before dropping the paddle.

The Cape Fear and Neuse River basins represent the largest and third-largest basins in the state, thus it seems fitting to conclude this section with a historically-highlighted focus on each namesake river. The Neuse basin measures 6,235 square miles of drainage area, all entirely within North Carolina, whereas the Cape Fear drains a massive 9,149 square miles before entering the Atlantic Ocean at Southport.

The Neuse runs 227 miles from Falls Lake in Raleigh to the Pamilco Sound along the coast and the Mountains-to-the-Sea paddle trail is a great resource for picking your launch site. A local favorite for the author is Cliffs of the Neuse State Park in Goldsboro, once a ceremonial ground and gathering place for the Tuscarora and Saponi tribes. Later in the 1700s, early European settlers set up a trading center at what is now known as Seven Springs. The cliffs of the park are a rainbow of white, tan, yellow and brown, rising approximately 90 feet above the water. Formed millions of years ago when a fault in the earth's crust shifted, they remain virtually unaltered and stand as a journal of the biological history of the area. Once you pass through Wayne County and the park area, the upstream section makes for a great inland wilderness paddle. The put-in at the NC 111 bridge to take out at Seven Springs is approximately 8 miles, but requires shuttle. As an alternative, you can launch from the park and paddle upstream at your leisure for a round trip.

While trekking along the Neuse, drop by the CSS Neuse State Historic Site along the waterfront in Kinston. Built in an effort to recapture Union-held New Bern during the Civil War, the ironclad gunboat was set afire in March of 1865. It was then sunk to avoid capture after its rebel crew shelled the advancing Union Cavalry. Another convenient paddling opportunity would be the least developed section of Johnston County from the SR 1201 bridge to the SR 1224 crossing in Wayne County, which is only a couple of miles, but puts you in the vicinity of the infamous Bentonville Battlefield. Fought during March 19-21, 1865, history buffs see this largest battle on North Carolina soil as being the last full-scale Confederate offensive from General Joseph Johnston as he attempted to block Union General William Tecumseh Sherman's march to Goldsboro.

The Cape Fear transcends much of the eastern Piedmont to the coast, and if you put in at Greensboro you can conceivably paddle all the way to the Atlantic. I don't recommend it unless you enjoy jumping over dams along the way, but there are several segments worthy of a family outing that deserve mention. Section One of the *Cape Fear Canoe Trail* is primarily flatwater, and enables you to pass by the area of a bridge erected by the redcoats of General Cornwallis during the American Revolution.

William D. Auman

Put-in lies at the US 1 bridge over the Deep River, and take-out would be the NC 42 access area, a distance of approximately 8 miles.

Section two of the river is a stretch of some 16 miles, beginning at the NC 42 access and ending at the SR 2016 take-out approximately 2 miles south of Lillington. This paddle is best accompanied by an overnight camp at Raven Rock State Park, which features hiking trails and a canoe-camp area. The upper reaches of section 2 include a portage around the abandoned Buckhorn Dam on the left, and a couple of class 2 rock gardens prior to reaching the park. The "rock" of the "Raven" was originally known as Patterson's Rock, so named after an early settler who found refuge there when his canoe capsized nearby. The name was changed in 1854 due to the inspiration of the numerous ravens that choose to roost along the ledges. If you paddle by, you can't help but marvel at the immense crystalline structure that rises to 150 feet and stretches for more than a mile along the river. In addition, the Rock of the Raven represents the dividing line between the Carolina Piedmont and Coastal Plain. Siouan and Tuscarora Indians hunted the area until the mid-1700s, and many arrowheads and pottery fragments have been discovered in the vicinity.

The best whitewater of the Cape Fear (yes there are rapids in the western coastal plain), can be found in section three. Begin at the SR 2016 access and paddle through the ledges until you reach the NC 217 bridge in Erwin *(*author's note: you can also put in at the county park just north of the bridge for an out-and-back upstream paddle)*. The rapids are largely the result of a major flood in 1865, which washed away several rock-filled wooden dams and locks that had been built by the Cape Fear Navigation Company. Their remains, together with a gradient that drops about 12 feet per mile, can be challenging to a novice paddler, so use caution. This paddle will take you to the vicinity of a legitimate ghost town, that being Averasboro, once the third-largest village in colonial North Carolina. Approximately 3 miles southwest of Dunn you will find the Averasboro Battleground, where Confederate General Hardee clashed with General Sherman's left flank three days prior to the battle at Bentonville. A new railroad came to the area in the 1880s, by-passing Averasboro but going directly through the heart of nearby Dunn. Such was the beginning of the end for a once flourishing little town.

These are but a few of the coastal plain area paddling voyages that our state has to offer, but each is unique in their inherent combination of accessibility and wilderness "feel." The majority can be considered suitable for a short family day trip, yet offer the option of more lengthy exploration. Hence, they qualify for author's choice, but are not exclusive in that other similar bodies of water exist within the area that can become "reader's choice." I would encourage you to explore available resources for more variety of experiences within this region, but for now we must head west towards our foothills and majestic mountains.

William D. Auman

Section Four: From Boone's Backyard to the waters of the Iswa

Although he will best be remembered for his frontier epic encounters and his Kentucky rifle, if Daniel Boone had not followed the Yadkin River upstream then who knows when Cumberland Gap might have been discovered? Boone came south from Pennsylvania with his family when his father Squire secured a warrant that claimed 640 acres in an area known as Forks of the Yadkin back in the fall of 1750. Some locals say that the Boones lived in a cave on the east side of the Yadkin during their first few months before building a cabin along Lickon Creek in present-day Davie County. It is remarkable to paddle past Boone's Cave State Park and climb the wooden staircase up from the river to the cave, which is approximately 80 feet long and very narrow. At the top you will also find a gravestone inscribed "Boone", but it is uncertain just which pioneer relative was laid to rest within the park. Legend also has it that Daniel himself used the cave as a hideout from the *Yattken* Indians, a small Siouan tribe that inhabited the foothills. A probable relative of the Catawba, the name translates into *"place of big trees."*

The Daniel Boone Heritage Canoe Trail is easy to research online and allows for a 22-mile voyage where one can experience ten distinct sections of the Yadkin, some of which have moderate whitewater. Among those, section three features Boone's Shoal-Big Rock rapid located just upriver from Dutchman's Creek, where newlyweds Daniel and Rebecca Boone

Pioneer Paddles of the Colonial South

once had a homesite. The cave appears on section six, but continue downriver to the Baptism Rock Access to disembark due to the steep embankment and stairway. High Rock Lake, which offers nice views of the Uwharrie mountains to the east and is bordered by game lands and mature forest, marks the end of the trail.

Yet another local tale insists that nearby Bear Creek was named from the season that Boone killed ninety-nine bears along its waters. This scenic creek, which is slightly southeast of the Uwharries in Moore County and close to the pottery capital of Seagrove, offers a nice paddle of about 2 miles. A favorite access point lies at the end of Carter's Mill Road just north of Robbins, and we have taken out many times just before the remains of historic Reynolds Mill *(built by the father of Judge Rufus W. Reynolds, North Carolina's first federal bankruptcy judge whom I am proud to call my Uncle)*. An alternate put-in at the NC 705 bridge in Robbins will add about a mile to the trip, which takes you through an area of little development and abandoned mill sites.

If you have time, visit the "House in the Horseshoe" a few miles to the east on the Deep River, home of former Governor Tom Benjamin Williams (1751-1814), a distant ancestral relative of the author. The colonial home, built in 1770 by Philip Alston, is one of but a few remaining structures in the nation where you can see actual bullet holes from a Revolutionary War skirmish. On July 29, 1781, British loyalists led by Commander David Fanning attacked Alston and his band of Patriots. Alston was forced to surrender after the British attempted to set fire to his home with a cart of burning straw.

William D. Auman

Williams, who served under George Washington in the 2nd N.C. Continental Regiment, bought the home in 1798 prior to his initial election as governor the following year. He served in that capacity from 1799-1802, and again from 1807-1808.

A short jaunt downstream takes us into the Uwharrie National Forest, a wilderness oasis within the foothills region. There we find Badin Lake, another man-made creation from the legendary Yadkin, which serves as a cousin to High Rock Lake. The Uwharries actually represent the oldest "mountain" range in the world, thought to have been formed approximately 300 million years ago. Although High Rock Mountain sits as the highest point at an elevation of 1,188 feet, the mountains give an appearance of being at a seemingly higher elevation since the valleys fall far below. As a comparison, the City of Asheville was built on a valley floor with an elevation of 2,134 feet, which seems low when compared to the surrounding mountains that range upwards of 6,000 feet. Although the 50,189 acres of the Uwharrie National Forest make it the smallest national forest in North Carolina, the forest service contends that it offers more archaeological sites per acre than any other in the southeastern United States.

Even the iconic John Lawson , the same original resident of Bath Town who sailed to the Carolina Coast in August of 1700, has ties to this region. He decided to venture into the unknown and potentially hostile backcountry by canoe with an Indian guide, as little was known of the Native American inhabitants of the area. In late January 1701, Lawson and his entourage of five Englishmen and various guides crossed into North Carolina in the neighborhood of present-day Charlotte, then the land of the Catawba. Continuing a northerly trek, on February 5, 1702, his party crossed the Uwharrie River *(recorded as "Heighwaree" by Lawson)* and came upon the village of Keyauwee Town.

If you wish to follow the Lawson route, access areas for Badin Lake can be found in both Montgomery and Stanley counties. Morrow Mountain State Park lies just to the southwest of the impoundment, creating a corridor of forest on both sides of what is now called the Pee Dee River. For some reason, the Yadkin changes its name when it leaves the Badin Dam, but keep going south and you will reach the third cousin in the chain of lakes, that being Lake Tillery. Access areas are offered on both the eastern and western shorelines, and it is easy to find the private nooks and crannies that only a paddler can appreciate. We enjoy the Dennis Road public access of the lower Uwharrie River, which begins just east of the Lake Tillery channel and allows for a short paddle to the mouth of the river.

Keep in mind that Boone's Yadkin (aka Pee Dee) is the connector from High Rock Lake to Tillery, and that wildlife access areas are easy to be located at points in between. A notable historical site near the town of Mt. Gilead is the *Town Creek Indian Mound*, which offers a glimpse into an excavated pre-Columbian settlement along Little River. Artifacts found in the area date back to the eleventh century.

While the Pee Dee continues its journey into South Carolina and on to the Atlantic Ocean, our epic pioneer (Mr. Boone that is) gained fame from going the opposite direction in an unconventional manner known as "poling." Poling what was likely a poplar dugout canoe upstream against the current all the way to the headwaters of the Yadkin near present-day Blowing Rock must have been a grueling experience. No doubt he traveled through one of his namesake towns known now as Boonville, and skirted the Mt. Airy hometown of actor Andy Griffith. He may have camped at nearby Pilot Mountain, known as "Mount Pilot" to Mayberry residents. The latter areas are considered part of the Sauratown Mountain Range, slightly larger than the Uwharries yet smaller than the Appalachians. I was somewhat surprised to learn that Myers Lake only exists within the creative minds of the television series, but a nearby paddle along a neighboring river is a worthwhile alternative.

The river of reference is the Dan, another topographical tribute to the infamous pioneer, located about a half-hour's drive to the north of Winston-Salem. Hanging Rock State Park in Stokes County offers public access to the Dan River, and it is approximately 5.5 miles from the park to take out at Moratock Park Access near Danbury. This stretch features high rocky bluffs and caves to explore with a "mountain feel" and clear water. You would never guess that the triad metropolitan area was nearby. Other access points can be found along the Dan River State Trail through an internet search.

Revisiting the Yadkin a final time, another paddle to consider would be the stretch from the Grandin Road bridge in Caldwell County to the end of Wilkes County Rt. 1137 on Kerr Scott Lake, a distance of approximately nine miles. You can shorten the Grandin to Kerr voyage to about five miles by putting in at the bridge in Ferguson. Another Boone family home was located nearby on the tributary of Beaver Creek, about

Pioneer Paddles of the Colonial South

three-fourths of a mile north of the river. Unless you wish to drag your boat under a draping canopy of forested tree limbs, as did the author, I would not suggest any attempt to venture upstream on Beaver Creek. Since the Yadkin ends, or rather begins, prior to reaching the bustling town of Boone, we must switch gears and adjust paddles to yet another river of colonial and pioneer legacy: the New.

It must have been somewhat ironic to Peter Jefferson, the father of Thomas, that what he would call the New River is actually thought to be the world's second oldest river after the Nile. Peter, who visited the area as a surveyor in 1749, is credited with having given the New its current name. Originating in Ashe County near the Virginia border, this section of river is predominantly calm and thus very conducive to family paddling. A 26 mile stretch that includes sections in both states makes for a quality overnighter with a stop at New River State Park (featuring paddle-in campsites), but other opportunities for day trips abound.

A favorite trek from years back begins at the NC 1560 bridge northeast of Boone near the community of Todd. Put-in is actually on the South Fork of the New, but the river merges with the North Fork northeast of Jefferson just past Twin Rivers Campground. You will pass the state park during this voyage of approximately 9 miles to Mouth of Wilson, Virginia, with signs clearly visible from the water. It is not uncommon to startle whitetail deer along the shoreline of this relatively undeveloped region. The community of Todd features a "throwback" general store that deserves a visit, and several outfitters operate in the area should you desire to customize your journey and maximize your time.

Another section of note along the South Fork begins at the US 221 bridge, which although not an optimum access point, leads to a tranquil paddle with two low-water bridges between the put-in and take out at NC 1179. You could also continue to the NC 163 bridge for take-out, but that adds 9.5 miles to what is otherwise an approximate 5 mile trip. The rainbow trout were hitting on spinnerbaits back in 1992, and beaver were encountered both then and in 1994, which I regret to say was the last official visit by the author to date. On that trip my friend David left the keys to our take-out vehicle at the put-in, so we had to hitchhike back in the bed of a farmer's hay truck! It's past time to get reacquainted with the New and bring the fishing rod! Smallmouth and "redeye" rock bass also await the angling paddler.

Many other options for day trips can be found along the New, and trip information can be easily obtained from local outfitters in the vicinity of Jefferson. Several private campsites are located riverside in places such as Glendale Springs, Piney Creek, Crumpler and West Jefferson, awaiting exploration by adventuresome families.

Time to shift gears and offer a footnote to the Central Piedmont, otherwise defined as the triangle to the east (Raleigh/Durham/Chapel Hill), the triad (Greensboro/Winston-Salem/High Point) to the south, and Charlotte Metro to the southwest. This area is host to approximately eighty percent of our state's populous, but does offer a quadrant of paddling turf worthy of mention. To be fair, this author has spent more time in

Pioneer Paddles of the Colonial South

search of wilderness waterways elsewhere in the Old North State, but on occasion has discovered some voyages of respite from the hustle and bustle that typifies the metro region, often when visiting family in the vicinity.

One such paddle worthy of inclusion would be Mountain Island Lake. This small gem of the piedmont is an impoundment of the Catawba River, located approximately 5 miles south of busy Lake Norman. Just across from the entrance you can take a walk around Hopewell Presbyterian Church, the final resting place of John McKnitt Alexander (1733-1817), one of the principal founding fathers behind the Mecklenburg Declaration of Independence and yet another ancestral uncle of the author, I am proud to say! John Adams and many notable scholars were convinced that Thomas Jefferson drew largely from this document of May 20, 1775 when drafting our national declaration, a premise addressed by other authors. As regards the lake, canoe access points are located in Latta Plantation Park in Mecklenburg County, home to the Carolina Raptor Center, which features everything from rescued bald eagles to owls and turkey vultures. Located less than 30 minutes from the Queen City, Latta serves as a tranquil measure of escape from the urban entrapment of the Charlotte metropolis. Gar Creek access is on the left near the end of Sample Road just past the Raptor Center, and North Shore access can be found with a right turn off of Sample Road just prior to the Center.

Within the plantation park you will still find a good deal of undeveloped shoreline with an occasional Osprey nest. Many trails cross through the mature woodlands, and whitetail deer are often encountered. Mountain Island itself is uninhabited and less than a one mile paddle from the North Shore put-in. A great spot for the young paddler to dinosaur hunt, which is what our grandchildren enjoy often from upstream access points on the Catawba at both Cowan's Ford and Eucia.

Cowan's Ford, with an accesss point just off of NC 73, was where on February 1, 1781, General Nathaniel Greene and his 800 Patriot troops attempted to stymie the advance of British General Lord Cornwallis through what was then North Carolina backcountry. Although considered a British victory with the loss of Patriot General William Davidson, Greene was successful in his endeavor to avoid a full-scale battle with the larger British force of roughly 2,400 men. Today only about a half-mile south of the access point we find Princess Island (named in honor of our granddaughters of course) that is easy to disembark upon prior to circumnavigating on a historical day trip. Eucia Access is also in close proximity to the south and offers a short paddle on Johnson Creek to the Catawba through the Cowan's Ford National Wildlife Refuge.

While in the Charlotte area, don't miss the U.S. National Whitewater Center (city folk do enjoy a few spoils every now and then!). You can marvel as Olympic hopefuls tackle the artificial whitewater course or drop your own paddle at the Catawba River access point near the South Trail. With over 1.5 miles of river frontage along the Catawba, the Center provides excellent opportunities for paddlers of all skill levels. Long Creek serves as the northern boundary of the Center and is easy to explore. In addition, the South Fork River is only a short paddle from the Catawba Access and features numerous tributary creeks accessible only via canoe or kayak.

Pioneer Paddles of the Colonial South

Although you can't paddle to it, colonial history buffs should take time to visit the *Rock House* while in the vicinity of our Queen City, which can be found at 3500 Shamrock Drive in the eastern section of town. The former home of Hezekiah Alexander (a brother to John McKnitt), who supervised the raising, provisioning, and financing of area Patriot forces during the American Revolution, is among the few remaining Revolutionary War era structures in the piedmont. It may also be the oldest free-standing, documented Masonic structure in the nation.

Let's continue with the Catawba, which is the namesake of yet another historical Native American tribe, originally known as *Iswa, "people of the river."* During the time of McKnitt and Hezekiah, as many as 5,000 tribal members lived along the river banks near what was then known as Charlottetown. In contrast to the approach taken by many indigenous peoples, the Catawba became fast allies with the colonial English, even joining them against the French, Cherokee, and others during the French and Indian War. North of Lake Norman, in the Hickory and Morganton areas, many additional Catawba River access points can be found to allow for trips of varying duration.

The Catawba River Basin begins on the eastern slopes of the McDowell County mountains and flows southeast through North Carolina until reaching the state border at Lake Wylie. The 224 mile river includes a chain of seven man-made lakes, and its longest free-flowing stretch covers only about 17 miles. Although perhaps the most densely populated basin within the state, the upper reaches of this history laden river are still quite pristine.

William D. Auman

At Quaker Meadows near Morganton, the mountain men responsible for the American Revolutionary War victory at Kings Mountain camped along the banks of the Catawba, a mere 7 days before the epic battle that served as a turning point in the war. On October 7, 1780, after riding all night and fording the swollen Broad River, the mountaineers with their long rifles either killed or captured the entire Loyalist army in less than an hour. This victory is widely regarded as the catalyst for America's ultimate triumph in the war, which ended a mere 12 months and 12 days later when Cornwallis surrendered to Washington at Yorktown. There is an easy 5 mile paddle with ripples of mild whitewater from Greenlee Ford Access to Rocky Ford in Morganton that features a bike trail along the river for shuttle on the path where the Patriots marched back in the day.

Before we continue our trek west, both Lake James and the South Fork of the Catawba offer prime options for paddling excursions. Many will remember James Fenimore Cooper's frontier saga known as the *Last of the Mohicans*, and a significant number of scenes from the movie were filmed in and around Lake James. On the Linville side of the lake, near where the fort was constructed for the film, the North Fork Access area showcases beautiful vistas of Hawksbill, Table Rock, Shortoff, and Brown Mountain. The latter is known as being home to the mysterious Brown Mountain Lights, which have intrigued visitors for centuries. Keep an eye peeled toward the northeast Blue Ridge and watch for what some describe as a glowing ball of fire.

The lights date back to Native American mythology as early as the year 1200. According to Cherokee legend, a great battle between the Cherokee and Catawba occurred at that time, and the lights represent the spirits of Indian maidens who continue to search through the centuries for those slain in the ancient battle. Other legendary accounts include that of the slave who continues to search for his planter/owner from the low country who became lost while hunting. Yet another involves a woman who was allegedly murdered by her husband back in 1850, and her ghost continues to haunt the mountain to this day. It has been confirmed that years later, a skeleton of the missing woman was found under a cliff along the mountainside!

The "first" lost colony of North Carolina is also found within the Upper Catawba River Valley. Lesser known than its English cousin to the east, Spanish conquistador Juan Pardo built Fort San Juan at a location along Upper Creek near the ancestral river town of Joara. The year was 1567, predating the Roanoke Island colony by two decades. Fort San Juan thereby enjoys the designation of being the earliest European settlement in the interior of what is now the United States. Fast forward to 1568, when only one Spanish survivor was left to attest that the fort had been overrun by the Catawba and burned to the ground. Now known as the Berry site, archaeologists from Warren Wilson College are continuing to excavate and uncover the mysteries of this lost colony with the assistance of volunteers such as myself and my wife.

Not far from Upper Creek, the Linville River enters Lake James after leaving the gorge which also bears its name (pioneer William Linville and his sons were scalped in 1766 while exploring the area, but their legacy lives on perpetually through the namesake river and gorge). Linville River, however, represents more of a fishing as opposed to paddling option at this point. In this section of the modern-day frontier, Lake James is the place to put-in as it is quite amenable to the shoreline paddler. Consider a voyage to the mouth of the Linville, but remember to bring the rod and reel. On the east end of the lake, the Catawba's south fork enters and allows for ideal family paddling both upstream and down. Both private and public access areas are easily found near Marion. Take NC 226 north from I-40 and take a right on Hankins Road. After only a couple of miles, the lake will appear on the horizon.

Back to Morganton and the 21st century we go, so consider a paddle on the Johns River just north of town. A relatively unknown, yet easy to paddle river, the Johns originates in the Pisgah National Forest and drains Wilson's Creek, known to be a world-class trout stream. Put-in off NC 18/US 64, and you have about 1.5 miles to paddle downstream before confluence with the Catawba. If you continue, you will soon enter the impoundment of Lake Rhodhiss. Along the way you will experience a wilderness environment with many spots to fish or picnic. Now we continue to move west as the *Land of the Sky* awaits...

Pioneer Paddles of the Colonial South

Section Five: The Blue Ridge and Beyond

"…the river, always the river, the dark eternal river, full of strange secret time, washing the city's stains away…is flowing by us, by us, to the sea." Thomas Wolfe

No writer can arguably match the eloquent command that Asheville's native son maintained over the English language. Most certainly the former quote references the predominant river of the mountain region, our own French Broad, which was to Wolfe as the Mississippi was to a guy named Samuel Clemens. Deemed *Acgiqua (Long Man)* by the native Cherokee, our love for this river is likewise profound in that our primary home stood on its banks just south of Marshall for 35 years prior to the devastating floods brought by Hurricane Helene. September 27, 2024, will always be a day of infamy for our family and for many others who also suffered tragic losses due to the historic, biblical-level flooding, yet our heart will always hold a special place for the French Broad. We will revisit that majestic river towards the end of this chapter.

It seems befitting to conclude this chapter in the geographic area where the majority of my adult life has been spent, a region filled with whitewater rivers and pristine, blue-water lakes. The naturalist William Bartram befittingly described the area as being where one can behold a *"world of mountains piled upon mountains."* Native American origins can be traced archaeologically back to the Paleo-Indian nomadic period of 10,000-8,000 B.C. and throughout the centuries native cultures have relied upon the poplar dugout canoe to traverse the waterways of their ancestral Appalachians. Unlike Northeastern and Canadian tribes, the Cherokee did not have access to the numerous white birch trees that dominate the boreal northern forests. Thus, as opposed to the more nimble and lightweight birchbark canoe, the Southern Appalachians gave birth to the poplar dugout, a close cousin of the cypress dugouts from eastern North Carolina. At the Oconaluftee Indian Village on the Cherokee Reservation, you can observe the process of how native artisans re-create the dugout canoe.

It is amazing to consider that in 1735 the Cherokee inhabited approximately 40,000 square miles in the mountain region with of total of 64 towns and villages. They called the area *"Sha-Kon-O-Hey,"* the phonetic spelling for "Land of Blue Smoke." There are many varieties of family friendly adventures to be discovered in this wilderness paradise, from pristine flatwater lakes to fast moving whitewater rivers. If a dugout isn't handy, canoes or kayaks with a keel or shallow "v" hull configuration would be the best choice for the former. These are generally made of wood, fiberglass, or aluminum. Whereas virtually any material can be used for flatwater, whitewater requires a construction design that will not crack or puncture. Many varieties of plastic composites will suffice, with polyethylene being the most common.

Imagine yourself by the lake at dawn, that gray area between night and day when fog clings to the water and invokes a surreal aura amid the world waking around it. So what are you waiting for? Let's begin with a section of Jackson County known locally as "Little Canada." I'm not certain of the exact source that designated the area as such, but the region bears a striking resemblance to prototypical Canadian wilderness waterways. A total of four lakes connect the Tuckasegee River, with each impoundment featuring a unique paddling experience. Each lake was created on the east fork of the river back in the mid-1950s in an effort to provide hydroelectric power to the region.

Cedar Cliff Lake represents the first in the chain if you are moving from west to east and is easy to access. From Sylva, take NC 107 south a little over ten miles to the community of Tuckasegee. Take the next left on Shook Cove Road (SR 1135), which is just past the left on NC 281 (*281 takes you to the remaining three lakes), and Cedar Cliff will appear within minutes. There is an NC Wildlife Commission put-in that you can't miss, and a waterfall on the eastern edge of the lake serves as the boundary to Bear Lake. The Tuckasegee River emerges from the western edge of Cedar Cliff, and offers yet another paddling option with several access points along 107 as you head downstream to Cullowhee.

Bear Lake is first in line to reach if you take the NC 281 option, and represents the largest body of water in the chain, covering almost 500 acres. As the big brother of the group, it also has a greater degree of development and boat traffic. Accordingly, this author recommends that you continue on next door to Wolf Creek Lake, or further to the smallest impoundment known as Tanasee Creek Lake. Wolf Creek Lake is

William D. Auman

"Little Canada" offers pristine waters such as Cedar Cliff Lake

approximately three miles long and is a paddlers dream, with surrounding Pisgah National Forest and many tranquil spots to beach the boat. Tanasee is a miniature bookend of only about a mile in length, but rarely will you find much additional company on the water. Both Wolf Creek and Tanasee offer a cooling summer swim and a quiet alternative to the vehicular traffic of autumn leaf-lookers.

In the Little Canada community known as East LaPorte, also just off of NC 107 and about a mile from the 281 turnoff, you will find a most curious artifact of Native American lore known as the Judaculla Rock. This soapstone boulder is covered in petroglyphs, and can be reached via SR 1737, also known as Caney Fork Road. Locals say the rock bears the hand print of the Cherokee giant Judaculla, who could drink a stream dry with one gulp and used lightening as arrows for his immortal bow. The slant-eyed giant allegedly leaped down off a nearby mountain and scratched the rock with his seven-fingered hands. Archaeological excavations in the vicinity have revealed, among other finds, stone bowls and quarrying tools dating back to the Late Archaic Period of 3000-1000 B.C.

Continue south on 107 and the road begins to rise. Higher and higher you climb and all of a sudden the blue waters of Lake Glenville (aka Thorpe Reservoir) appear with a shoreline elevation of approximately 3,800 feet. Considered to be the highest major lake in eastern America, Glenville is 6 miles long with 26 miles of sandy shores to explore. A mixture of Pisgah National Forest and areas of development surround the lake, which features many islands and coves to discover. Peregrine Falcons roost on Whiteside Mountain, easily seen from the lake, where the mythical *Utlunta ("spear finger")* of Cherokee lore attempted to build a great rock bridge through the air to Hiwassee. His efforts were said to be thwarted by lightening, yet locals insist that remnants of the bridge can still be seen on Whiteside.

Since we can't utilize *Utlunta's* byway, our trek west must continue by road to a little known lake which feeds an infamous river of the same name—the Nantahala. Just south of the gorge, the lake is somewhat secluded with Nantahala National Forest on the western shore and limited development to the east. A few miles east of Andrews, it can be accessed from SR 1310 from the east and SR 1401 to the west via the adjoining forest service road. Bear hunting is prevalent within this area of national forest, so be aware and check your calendar for timing. One November many years ago we encountered a frightened raccoon swimming towards our canoe while attempting to escape from the barking blue tick hounds that it had left behind on the shore.

If you are in the mood for whitewater thrills, leave the lake and continue north into the "Land of the Noonday Sun" gorge and visit one of the area outfitters for a river run. The Nantahala Outdoor Center is a world-renowned training ground for Olympic paddlers, many of whom can be observed practicing their technique on any given day. For those who would rather stick to flat-water, Lake Santeelah is a short hop, skip, and jump to the northwest.

Santeelah is located off of US 129 in Graham County, just next to Robbinsville, a picturesque little town perhaps best known as a filming location for Jodie Foster's movie *Nell*. Chief Junaluska, the Cherokee hero credited with saving the life of Andrew Jackson at the Battle of Horseshoe Bend, is interred in the local cemetery. Ironically, Jackson later betrayed the Cherokee when he sanctioned Indian removal in 1838, a dark era for American history that came to be known as the *Trail of Tears*. Although Junaluska was forced to join his comrades in the march to Oklahoma, he returned to North Carolina on foot and in 1847 was awarded land in the Robbinsville vicinity. Together with Colonel William Thomas, he is credited with being primarily responsible for the recognition of the Cherokee

Pioneer Paddles of the Colonial South

Eastern Band. He died in 1868 at the ripe old age of 93.

Popular with paddlers, the lower section of Santeelah towards the Horse Cove camping area and Little Santeelah Creek avoids most of the motorboat traffic that can be found near Cheoah Point above the dam. There are many secluded spots to investigate, and the Snowbird Mountains to the South and Unicoi to the west foster an elegant alpine curtain that is difficult to reduce to a written description.

Although you can't paddle to it, when in the Santeelah area be sure to take the short drive to Joyce Kilmer Memorial Forest. From the lake, simply continue on SR 416 after passing Horse Cove and you will soon reach the picnic area. Set aside in 1936 as a living memorial to the poet/soldier Kilmer, this forest is perhaps the most impressive example of original, old-growth in the eastern United States. An easy 2-mile loop trail winds through the towering trees, many of whom are over 100 feet tall and over 20 feet in circumference. At many spots on the forest floor you can see remnants of the massive American Chestnut trees that dominated the forest prior to the blight which began in 1925. According to Cherokee legend, when the earth was created the abundant Frazier Fir and Hemlock were among the species that did not fall asleep. Accordingly, they remain evergreen year round. Even now, this virgin wilderness remains a place of inspiration and contains a treasure trove of native flora and fauna.

Canoe "purists" will always rave, and justifiably so, about the Boundary Waters Wilderness of the Minnesota Canadian border. North Carolina, however, can also boast of its own boundary water--that being Calderwood Reservoir which straddles our own Swain County and the Blount County, Tennessee line. Put in at Tapoco just off 129 below the Cheoah Dam, and a paddle west will take you into Davey Crockett country in about a mile. What begins as Nantahala National Forest turns into Cherokee National Forest, with more isolation and remote wilderness than you will find just about anywhere else within the region. Several small waterfalls appear on the north shore of the lake as you paddle towards Slickrock Creek, the mouth of which lies just into the Tennessee side on the southern shore. The creek is navigable only for about a hundred yards, but a hiking trail runs alongside it and allows for a nice interlude to stretch your legs.

Calderwood is a short jaunt west from Fontana Lake (see discussion below) and north of Santeelah, and one would be remiss to bypass the splendor it offers when paddling within the area. Cheoah Reservoir adjoins Calderwood to the east and is likewise a popular paddling destination. Follow NC 28 west from Fontana and you will arrive at Cheoah in approximately 5 miles.

The Little Tennessee River, perhaps the most environmentally healthy river in the mountain region, enters Fontana on the south side after flowing through alternating farmlands and woodlands in both Macon and Swain counties. Rock hounds love the town of Franklin, formerly known as *Nikwasi* to the Cherokee, which is widely renowned for its gem mining and mineral deposits and features a 1,000+ year-old Cherokee mound that still stands in the middle of downtown. Take advantage of a calm paddle that winds through the town courtesy of a local greenway, or venture beyond into mild whitewater that leads past the site of the ancient Cherokee town of *Cowee ("wolf-clan place")*.

If the former appeals to you, put in at Big Bear Park located on Northeast Main Street, where you will also find picnic shelters and a playground for the kids. The 1540 De Soto expedition crossed the Little Tennessee in this area, and it is approximately a 3 mile paddle along the greenway to the Nonah Bridge just off the US 64 Bypass/US 441 overpass. An alternative route with a genuine wilderness feel would be to put in at the NC 28 bridge at Iotla for a ten mile run to Lost Bridge. It's not hard to locate a grassy bank suitable for canoe camping along this stretch if you wish to break up the trip.

Cowee was located in this vicinity, and visible evidence of ancient fish weirs can be seen just north of town where the river rejoins NC 28. Both the Cherokee and the frontier pioneers would herd fish through the open end of the "V" rock structures into waiting nets, which was less challenging than today's fly rod, but likely more productive!

An additional 13 miles brings you to Fontana Lake, however this section of river can be quite difficult, especially when lake levels are low. My advice would be to utilize the roof racks on your canoe-mobile and drive to the US 19 bridge just southwest of Bryson City. A flat-water paddle can begin here, or at backwater access areas where either the Nantahala or Tuckasegee Rivers enter the lake. A favorite launching pad lies on the campground side within the *Tsali* Recreation Area, known for its premier mountain bike trails. Put in on Mouse Branch

William D. Auman

Creek and you'll reach the main body of the lake in about a mile and a half. The Great Smoky Mountains National Park dominates the north shore of Fontana, while the Nantahala National Forest covers much of the southern shore.

Tsali ("Charlie"), represents more than just the name of a canoe station, and his legend remains an inspiration to the Cherokee people. Under the terms of the 1836 Treaty of New Echota, all Cherokee were required to give up their homeland and move to the west of the Mississippi River. Tsali, who had not been privy to the treaty process, was living at the time with his wife and three children in a cabin near the mouth of the Nantahala River. Soldiers arrived at his home during the summer of 1838, evicted the family and marched them towards Bushnell Stockade (now covered by the waters of Fontana). Accounts differ as to how and why, but all agree that an altercation occurred while en route to the stockade, resulting in the death of at least one soldier.

Tsali escaped and a manhunt ensued, resulting in the eventual capture and execution of several Cherokee. Tsali's wife and youngest son were spared, but a total of four, including Tsali himself, were tied to a tree and shot. It was widely reported that Tsali had surrendered so that federal troops would leave his beloved mountains and allow his kinsmen, many of whom were hiding in area caves and "hollars", to remain in their homeland. No doubt the spirits of these heroic men still wander the shores of Fontana. Without such sacrifice, it is likely that the stage would never have been set for recognition of the Eastern Band of Cherokee.

Pioneer Paddles of the Colonial South

Perhaps the most beautiful lake east of the Mississippi, Fontana has 240 miles of shoreline and covers over 10,500 acres. Dam construction began in 1942, and in 1944 the lake began to fill. The entire town of Judson was submerged, and many valley homes and farms were flooded. Accordingly, the ghosts of pioneers past are said to be seen alongside the artifacts of their existence, forever lost and wandering the deep waters of the lake.

Many access areas can be found along the lake shore, from Alarka on the east to Fontana Village on the western edge, but be cognizant of the motorboat traffic that will likely share in at least the beginning of your journey. A personal favorite somewhat off the grid is the Wilderness access area in the Roundhill Community just west of Bryson City. From there it is about a two mile paddle to the mouth of Forney Creek along the north shore, which is a great spot for a picnic, hike, or overnight canoe camp.

This area of the national park is quite remote and we have often seen tracks of the park's signature mammal, the black bear *("Yanegwa" in Cherokee),* while exploring the creek bed. Several years ago we even spotted a bear relocation cage a few yards off the trail! Bears, like their brethren alligator to the east, are the kings of their environment yet generally afraid of humans. An occasional attack within the region is reported, so take necessary precautions, but don't let unwarranted phobia keep you away from the jewel that is Fontana Lake.

Another western gem that includes an ancient legend would be Lake Hiawasee in the southwestern corner of our Old North State near Murphy. The spot where the Valley River meets

William D. Auman

the Hiawassee is known among the Cherokee as *Tianusi'yi, or "Leech place."* Just above the junction on the Valley is a deep hole and above it a ledge of rock that people used to use as a bridge. One day an enormous red object was seen lying on the ledge which unrolled and stretched itself out along the rock before disappearing from sight within the deep waters of the river. The water then began to boil and foam and a great column of white spray erupted high into the air where the men had been standing, but they had moved in timely fashion and then ran away to safety. Others would later find bodies lying along the bank with ears and nose eaten off until people became afraid to traverse the bridge. One day a young brave decided to paint his face, put on his finest buckskin, and tackle the bridge while singing *"Tianu'si gae'ga digi' gage Dakwa'nitlaste'sti: ("I'll tie red leech skins on my legs for garters")*. Others watched from a distance and when he was halfway across the river the water began to boil, a great wave rose and carried him downstream never to be seen again.

I have yet to see the Great Leech when putting in on Payne Street in Murphy, where you can paddle both upstream approximately a mile along the undeveloped shoreline of the Valley or downstream about a mile on the Hiwasee to another access point. If you do opt for either option, be apprised that other stories of the leech abound and perhaps it would be a good idea not to sing.

There was a time when people came to the mountains to breathe the fresh air, enjoy the spectacular scenery, and experience a lifestyle quite the opposite from that which they had grown accustomed. Today, although development has had its impact, there is still a place where mountain breezes blow unfettered through the trees, and where one of the most historic rivers in the world still flows as it always has, through forest, field and mountain valley. That would be the French Broad, aka *Acgiqua,* one of several places where the mythical world of the mountains still comes alive.

      Tears come to my eyes as I write this section of the book, as September 27, 2024 will forever be a day of infamy for myself, our family, and many others. Hurricane Helene wrecked unparalleled devastation along the French Broad, claiming lives and forever altering the river valley through a biblical level of flooding that destroyed our family home of 35+ years. We miss our tranquil existence roughly 5 miles south of Marshall, the Madison County seat which saw the river rise to 27 feet, 19 feet above flood stage, yet property can be replaced whereas lives cannot. Time passes, memories remain and resilient souls will rebuild as the river still flows.

      Native American legend has it that the *Nunnehi*, a race of immortal spirits, inhabit rock caves along the river. They are the "little people", barely reaching up to a man's knee in height, but well-shaped and handsome with long hair flowing almost to the ground. They are charged with protecting the French Broad and other mountain rivers from those who would bring harm to the ecosystem. No doubt that Iron Eyes Cody has frequently utilized their assistance during his lifelong battle against pollution.

      The French Broad will be forever memorialized in the treatise of the same name written by the late Wilma Dykeman,

William D. Auman

first published in 1955. This author would be doing the reader a disservice by attempting to provide a comparable history when such a comprehensive account is still in print and readily available. Consequently, we will focus on the many sections of the river that offer the modern day pioneer a variety of 21st century wilderness encounters. Do keep in mind, however, that Hurricane Helene had a significant impact on the river and confirm accessibility prior to planning your trek.

Acgiqua carves its way through the rugged slopes of some of the earth's oldest mountains, winding a total of 117 miles through North Carolina's share of the Appalachians. Hernando De Soto's expedition passed through the area in 1540 while searching for gold, and there remains today a legend of a cave laden with silver that overlooks the river at Hot Springs. If you take out or put in at Hot Springs, be sure to hike the Silvermine Trail up to Lover's Leap and take a dip in the natural mineral hot tubs upon return (see additional discussion later in the chapter).

Early European settlers bestowed upon the river its current name, largely because it flowed northwest into what was then French territory. In the 1780s, the first English settlers crossed the Blue Ridge, with Samuel Davidson settling above the Swannanoa River, a tributary of the French Broad that is likewise navigable by canoe when water levels are up. Davidson was reportedly killed by a Native American hunting party, and his grave lies just off a Warren Wilson College trail on a ridge above the river. The Swannanoa can be accessed at the college, only a few miles from US 70 east of Asheville. From there to Recreation Park in Asheville the paddle is about 11 miles through predominately wooded areas and farmland. If you take out at the US 70 bridge at Azalea, the trip can be shortened to about 8 miles. Do keep in mind, however, that Hurricane Helene wreaked havoc along the Swannanoa in September of 2024 as well, so be sure to check current conditions before launching.

The Swannanoa, a "chattering child of the Long Man," flows into the French Broad just south of downtown after a run through both urban areas and Biltmore Estate property. The Biltmore Avenue bridge in South Asheville can be a makeshift access option to avoid the former, and allows for a forested 2.5 mile paddle to Jean Webb Park on the French Broad. About a half-mile before its confluence there used to be a sandy beach stopping point that was named "Bill's Beach" by the author, complete with signage, however the topography was significantly modified in the wake of Helene's destruction. There went my chance for claiming a part of the Biltmore Estate by the legal doctrine known as adverse possession! Do keep in mind that the Swannanoa is a narrow stream with many downed trees ("strainers"), and is also susceptible to water level impediments. The best time for paddling is generally the spring, especially when the dogwoods begin to bloom.

From Champion Park near its headwaters in Rosman, to Newport, Tennessee, the French Broad was designated a North Carolina River Trail in 1987. This was the first such designation by our state. In 2012, non-profit organizations partnered with government to form the official French Broad River Paddle Trail, which I would encourage prospective paddlers to review online, particularly in light of the impact that Helene has had on various access points. Generally a placid, flat-water stream south of Asheville, the river changes character after leaving the big city. Whitewater, both mild and that worthy of portage, begins to coincide with *Acguiqua's* exit from the metro area. The Cherokee called this section of the river *"Tahkeyostee" ("where they race"),* and many outfitters offer rafting trips along the Class III to V rapids of section 9 in Madison County.

For family-oriented solace and calm water, begin near the upstream terminus. Try the put-in at Champion Park in Rosman, just off NC 64 along Old Rosman Road. It is a mere 2.5 miles to the access at Lyon's Mountain Road, and another 5 miles to the vicinity of the kind folks at Headwaters Outfitters. Island Ford Road access is yet another 2 miles, so many take-out options exist. This section represents the beginning of the "Long Man", as the East, West, and North Forks of the river all merge together in Rosman. The river is quite narrow through this stretch as it meanders through farm country with an occasional long range mountain view.

Another familiar run begins at Island Ford in Transylvania County (yes, potential vampires most certainly do abound, especially given that the landmark monolith known as Devil's Courthouse is nearby along the Blue Ridge Parkway). From Island Ford to Hap Simpson Park in Brevard the paddle is approximately 8 miles through a primarily calm and winding channel, but one never knows what adventure lies around the next bend. The site of the Island Ford access marks a historical pioneer crossing, and pieces of old wagons are sometimes seen when the river is low.

Pioneer Paddles of the Colonial South

The author's beach along the Swannanoa offered a nice respite from 1988-2024

     The following war story has to be worthy of inclusion. During the late '90s on a warm spring day, our family of four decided to explore the aforementioned section of river for the first time. I'm taking a break from paddling, having turned it over to the kids (ages 10 and 8 at the time), and had just cracked open a cold beer. All of a sudden I hear farmer Wilson yelling at us. "Come here, I need your help!" he bellowed towards our approaching vessel. "Excuse me?" was all I could muster. For all I knew, he could have been the father of Eric Rudolph or possibly some relative of the Deliverance movie cast.

     "My cow is giving birth and the calf is breached." Well, that ruled out Rudolph and the enemies of Burt Reynolds, but it was my grandparents and not I that had grown up on a farm.

William D. Auman

Turns out that farmer Wilson needed help to insert the rope around the calf, then pull it out. If not, no doubt both mother and baby wouldn't make it. To shorten the tale, both myself and our wide-eyed kids watched as my wife (a people nurse, not a vet), inserted the rope and tied it off. After that enlightening educational experience, Mr. Wilson and I were able to yank out baby Bessie. We visited for a time, said our goodbyes, and continued on our journey. No vampires or dinosaurs, but definitely a trip that will be remembered by all.

The Transylvania region is known as the "land of the waterfalls", and features the Estatoe Trail, a Cherokee "highway" that linked mountain settlements with the town of the same name in South Carolina. The trail crossed the state line near Rosman, and passed through the county seat of Brevard. Near the Hannah's Ford access, at a place called Bunker Hill, a skirmish is said to have been fought in 1811. This was part of an ongoing land dispute between both Carolinas and Georgia, and was known as the Walton War. At some point John Boy apparently said good night and the boundaries were ultimately settled.

The French Broad continues its northwesterly flow downstream from Transylvania into Henderson County, then veers to the east for several miles. The river is still bordered largely by agricultural bottom land, with the first river access being at Blantyre, found off of SR 1503 and just a short distance from US Hwy 64. It is about 10.5 river miles to the first take-out at Johnson Bridge off Banner Farm Road, and another 2 miles to Kings Road access on NC 191. From Kings Road, Westfeldt River Park is an approximate 6 mile paddle.

Pioneer Paddles of the Colonial South

Another stretch of flat-water takes us from Henderson County to Buncombe, with access points beginning at Glenn Bridge River Park, also off of 191 and about 2 miles from Westfeldt. After reaching Glenn Bridge, the river runs parallel to Interstate 26 for most of its 5.5 mile trek to Bent Creek River Park, which lies next to the Blue Ridge Parkway and across from the North Carolina Arboretum. Additional access points can be found at Hominy Creek, Amboy Park, Jean Webb Park and the Craven Street bridge in the heart of Asheville's river district, which will ultimately recover from the hurricane and be as vibrant as before. Be prepared for company on this "metro" area paddle due to its popularity with the visiting tubers.

The Bent Creek to Hominy paddle of approximately 6 miles takes you by George Vanderbilt's stunning mansion, the Biltmore House, which is America's largest privately owned residence. Vanderbilt (1862-1914), purchased approximately 125,000 acres of wilderness and constructed his palace on land that remains in the hands of his heirs to this day. In lieu of developing the remaining acreage, George saw fit to assist in preserving the majority of his property, resulting in the creation of modern-day Pisgah National Forest.

North of Asheville, above the dam in Woodfin, the waters of *Tahkeyostee* begin as the personality of the river begins its transformation. The little town of Woodfin features two river parks, Silver-Line and Riverside, a mile apart and next to NC 251, otherwise known as "river road." Riverside Park will soon be expanded to feature Taylor's Wave, a world-class artificial whitewater wave for the intermediate to advanced paddler. While located within a fairly developed district, it is possible to put-in at either park and paddle upstream for some smallmouth bass or muskie fishing. If you choose to venture downstream, however, be ready for some consistent Class III level whitewater. Ledges Whitewater Park is approximately 3.5 miles from Woodfin, with Walnut Island Park another 5 miles.

Although the river snakes its way between 251 and the Norfolk-Southern railroad, the municipal flavor of Jean Webb and Woodfin soon gives way to a wilderness feel. As many bicycles as vehicles enjoy the scenic road, which hugs the rocky cliffs of the French Broad River Gorge all the way to Marshall. Those motorists in a hurry generally take the 4-lane highway that runs parallel on the opposite side of the gorge, so the sounds of the river frequently sing solo. NC 251 was once part of the infamous Buncombe Turnpike, the principal thoroughfare for trade between South Carolina and Tennessee from the 1800s until the coming of the railroad.

Drovers road horseback along this former Indian path in front of immense numbers of cattle and hogs that were driven through the river valley for sale to seaboard markets. There was even an annual turkey drive, where thousands of the gobblers made way to upstate South Carolina for their ultimate date with a slaughterhouse. Tavern-keepers with hog stands set up shop along the turnpike, where they sometimes fed up to 100,000 hogs in a single day.

The Woodfin to Hot Springs stretch of river was home to stands at Alexander, Marshall, Barnard, and Stackhouse, offering the weary farmer respite in the form of poker and alcohol, together with an opportunity to fraternize with sometimes "nefarious" characters. The Civil War suspended railroad construction and thereby prolonged the utility of this rudimentary form of interstate commerce, but the rails were joined with their western link in 1882 at the Tennessee line. At that point it is said that the turnpike traffic ceased about as abruptly as it began.

  Returning to Walnut Island Park, the voyage to the mouth of the Ivy River is slightly less than 5 miles and represents "home court" to the author, having traversed this section of waterway well over a two-hundred times dating back to 1988, often with visiting friends or family. Each trip, however, fosters a unique experience all its own. As noted by Heraclius (540-480 B.C.), one "cannot step twice into the same river; for other waters are ever flowing on to you." Great blue heron, bald eagles and Canada geese frequently join us on this section, together with the occasional otter, beaver, or white-tailed deer.

  After a small rapid next to the park, the river is calm for about a half-mile with Sandy Mush Creek entering on the left. Paddle under the railroad trestle and stop for a drink while listening to the rushing water. Continue on and you cross into Madison County in less than a mile. The river makes a horseshoe turn at Bailey Bend (*locals call it "turkey neck curve"), named for the family of former Madison Sheriff Jesse James Bailey. Sheriff Bailey was in office during the time of prohibition, and waged a war on moonshiners that later became known as the era of Bloody Madison.

  Rock outcroppings with sheer faces known to some (yes,

William D. Auman

we named them after our kids back in the day) include Mariah's Lookout, Dylan's Ledge, and Falling Rock Gap, all appearing on river right after the bend. Moderate Class I-II whitewater interspersed with stretches of flatwater predominate until you reach Panhandle Shoals, about 2 miles south of the bend and about a half-mile from where our home once stood. If the river is high, it would be advisable to scout this area of rock garden, which is the only significant segment of white-water during the run. The Ivy appears on your right about a mile from Panhandle, and an easy roadside take-out on 251 is about 50 yards upstream of the confluence. Madco Tubing also has a takeout just below the mouth of the Ivy, so stop and say hello to Jim Hampton, their friendly proprietor, if time allows.

As an alternative, you can choose to continue on to the stairstep access at the community of Rollins (approximately another 2 miles), or take out just prior to the 8' Capitola Dam in Marshall about a mile from Rollins. Marshall, formerly known as Lapland, is the county seat of Madison with river on one side and mountain on the other. The town features an annual Mermaid Festival where the mystical creatures swim upstream from the Mississippi River all the way to the celebration in Marshall. Some ride on the beds of trucks or trailers during the parade, while others are able to grow legs temporarily and march before returning to the river and transforming back into their persona of the magical water nymph.

As noted by Wilma Dykeman, folks know Marshall as the town that is "a block wide, a mile long, sky high and hell deep." The town was devastated by Helene, but the resilient locals are bringing it back day-by-day. Madco Brew House is still serving thirsty paddlers their trademark craft beer on Main Street and gourmet coffee can be found at nearby Zuma's.

Sitting high above the Buncombe Turnpike we find Mariah's Lookout and Dylan's Ledge keeping watch over the French Broad River just north of Bailey Bend

Penlands, a landmark department store which first opened in 1926, is again selling local crafts, books and multitude of other items once again. Blannahassett Island sits in the middle of the river just next to downtown, and can serve as a put-in for a 2 mile moving water run to the 25' Redmon Dam if you so desire. From Redmon to Barnard, a trip of about 5.5 miles, consistent

William D. Auman

Class I-II whitewater takes you into forested wilderness and away from the highway.

Rafting expeditions rule the downstream section from Barnard to Stackhouse to Hot Springs, which is not recommended for open boaters or novice paddlers. This run of about 9 miles through Pisgah National Forest, does, however, offer some of the most remote river wilderness in western North Carolina. If you accept the challenge, a ghost town known as Runion awaits your exploration at the mouth of Big Laurel Creek. Big Laurel is also home to an expert-only level of whitewater, too extreme for this author to attempt to navigate, so we will continue to hike to Runion.

The trail can be found just off US 25/70 and leads to what was a logging camp village of approximately a thousand people at the turn of the 20th Century. Stone foundations nestled within the temperate rainforest jungle are all that remain of the once bustling community. Hot Springs awaits about 3 miles downstream on the French Broad, so be sure to take a soak in the natural thermal spa waters while in the area. The Nantahala Outdoor Center maintains a parking area for river access in this town of about 500 residents, and the open boater can enjoy the option of returning to the water here.

Formerly known as Warm Springs, the town served as headquarters for the Confederate Provisional Forces under General Davis during the Civil War, but was taken by federal troops in 1863. Earlier that same year, the cruelty of the war reached a dark pinnacle when a Confederate lieutenant colonel authorized the firing squad execution of what were thought to be

Pioneer Paddles of the Colonial South

Union sympathizers, one a mere 14 years of age. Known as the Shelton Laurel Massacre, the manhunt was in response to a series of break-ins that had occurred during the previous month in Marshall. Only food and necessary supplies had been stolen, and some of the helpless captives had not even been part of the raid. Such was not a time for due process.

If you choose to put-in alongside the many disembarking rafts at Hot Springs, set aside an hour or so to hike up the Silvermine Trail to Lover's Leap, where it joins the Appalachian Trail *(*author's note: the route of the latter, running from Georgia to its northern terminus in Maine, treks right through downtown Hot Springs).* The trail head is only a short walk from the Nantahala access, and the kids might just see a glint of silver from the long-lost mine along the way. Treasure hunters have searched for the entrance to the mine for many years, but to no avail. A panoramic river vista awaits at Lover's Leap, where, like many other spots found at various North American river valleys, an Indian maiden supposedly jumped after learning that her betrothed would not be coming back to her.

Shortly after you hit the river, on river-left you will see the spa grounds and foundational structures from days gone by when Hot Springs was a booming resort. The grounds even served as a German prisoner-of-war camp during World War I, and the detainees actually built cabins with intricate carpentry detail during their tenure of encampment. The river here is active, but manageable for a family venture with reasonable caution. Paint Creek Road runs along the eastern edge which allows for a bicycle shuttle if you are up for it. Only a few homes can be seen in the distance off shore as the river continues

William D. Auman

to bisect Pisgah National Forest.

    Murray Branch river access is about 4 miles downstream, and you will reach Paint Rock after another 2.5 miles. Named for the Native American drawings that have worn away to a large extent, the rock formation still stands tall as a remaining colonial boundary between North Carolina and Tennessee. In 1793, early settlers erected a blockhouse fortress here in an effort to provide protection from Indian attacks, and such appears on many maps from the pioneer era. At this point, Paint Creek enters the French Broad on river-right and Pisgah gives way to Cherokee National Forest.

    The French Broad now leaves North Carolina behind as it continues its journey to the Mississippi. Soon nothing will be left of *Tahkeyostee* wild water, and the gorge will eventually give way to farmland reminiscent of that found in the river headwaters. In fact, the river will soon settle into the 32,000 acre TVA impoundment known as Lake Douglas on the western edge of Newport. The French Broad does survive the spillway and winds through eastern Tennessee until joining with the Holston River just before entering the Knoxville area. Viola, the Tennessee River is born!

    In spite of our hurricane losses, we remain thankful for the river who has graced Western North Carolina with its presence for centuries; the river who, according to the Cherokee, rests its head on the mountains with its feet along the valleys, being fed by its chattering children; the river of our family during our time, and the river that waits for you and yours.

Pioneer Paddles of the Colonial South

CHAPTER THREE

Volunteers, Cavaliers, Peaches and Palmettos

Section One: Kings of the Wild Frontier in Tennessee

    I always admired Fess Parker, whether he was wearing his Davy Crockett or Daniel Boone coonskin cap. As a child I would often wander the woods pretending to be exploring along with Mingo and would particularly enjoy family trips to Cherokee where I would often bring back some "Made in China" version of a flintlock cap pistol or tomahawk. I guess those formative years had an impact on my pioneer paddling obsession that continues today?

    Since we left the previous chapter on the verge of entering Tennessee, it seems only appropriate to begin this excursion chapter with the Volunteer state. Rocky Top may not be home sweet home to me as the song goes, but it is a beautiful state that was carved out of North Carolina in 1796 after the latter had ceded its western lands to the federal government in 1789. Our primary paddling experiences are focused in the mountainous eastern region, which is an easy day trip from our western North Carolina home. One of our consistent favorites, a surprise to no one, would be the French Broad's upper access at Rankin Bridge and Leadvale at Douglas Lake just past Newport. Both of these sections are quite remote and relatively free from the motorboat traffic that is prolific as you head downstream towards the dam. From Rankin Bridge it is possible to paddle upstream past Clay Creek to the Fork Island section where the

William D. Auman

Pigeon River enters the French Broad, but the river soon changes character thereafter as the calm waters give way to ripples of whitewater that restrict further travel upstream. At the Rankin access you will find a gravestone of early settler Thomas Clark who passed in 1821, together with several other unmarked graves with dates unable to be deciphered.

Leadvale access is roughly a couple of miles downstream from Rankin and allows for an easy paddle across from an abandoned railroad trestle to several islands with sandy beach areas to break for a swim or artifact foray. The best time to hunt for arrowheads begins when the lake level is drawn down by the Tennessee Valley Authority toward the end of the summer. Obsidian, flint and most frequently quartz projectile points have been commonly found in the area. Leadvale also offers a choice to paddle about a mile upstream to explore McGowan Creek or to venture up the Nolichucky River from where it enters the lake.

The name "Nolichucky" was derived from the distortion of an old Cherokee area settlement called *No'natlugv'yi* which means "spruce tree place." From the mouth of the Nolichucky it is possible to navigate about a half-mile upstream before whitewater begins to greet you. If you were able to continue further you would eventually reach Davy Crockett Birthplace State Park in Limestone, which lies just above the river and is a perfect setting for camping. The legendary pioneer and congressman who met his demise at the Alamo in 1836 was born on this site, not on a mountaintop as the song says, back in 1786. He will always, however, be known as the King of the Wild Frontier. A 383-acre lake impounded by the Nolichucky Dam that bears his name can be found just 7 miles south of Greenville

Pioneer Paddles of the Colonial South

of off Tennessee Highway 152 and is another worthy venture for the paddler.

Davy was not the only "Fess Parker" to frequent haunts in Eastern Tennessee. Although his roots began near Reading, Pennsylvania and with his youth having been spent in the foothills of Western North Carolina, my ancestral neighbor known as Daniel Boone (*the author's paternal ancestry also originated near Reading and migrated to the Uwharrie Mountains of North Carolina roughly 30 years after Squire Boone came south in the 1750s) also has a notable history in the Volunteer state.

On March 10, 1775, Boone led his band of trailblazers from Long Island on the Holston River through Kingsport and beyond, traversing 200 miles of wilderness to the Cumberland Gap of Virginia. His namesake town of Boonesborough in Kentucky would come later, with hundreds of thousands of early settlers following the Gap through the Appalachians and to points further west. My wife actually found one of their musket balls while hiking the trail (which of course belonged to Daniel!). Boone and Richard Henderson had previously negotiated the Treaty of Sycamore Shoals at a site near Elizabethtown on the Watauga River that provided for purchase of Tennessee and Kentucky lands from the Cherokee, but some tribal members, together with the Shawnee who used these lands for hunting, remained in opposition to the sale. Jumping ahead, on September 25, 1780, the same site was used for mustering of the Overmountain Men, who later defeated the British on October 7 at the Battle of Kings Mountain, turning the tide in the Revolutionary War (see discussion in the NC chapter).

William D. Auman

Long before these settlers came to the river valleys of the Holston, Watauga, Clinch, Powell and Cumberland, a network of trails had been developed by Indigenous Peoples of the region. This system was known as *Athawominee* ("Great Warriors Path"), which later evolved into the Wilderness Trail. Although parts of the trail still remain, modern-day Interstates 26 and 81 follow the eastern leg of the path and Interstate 75 and US Hwy 25 follow the western leg. Although you can't paddle to it, according to the Tennessee Urban Forestry Council and local legend, "D.Boon cilled a bar in 1760" could be found carved into a beech tree just above an old Chickasaw Indian trail above what is now known as Boone's Creek. Our 26th President, Theodore Roosevelt, mentioned the tree in his book "The Winning of the West." The tree itself fell during a storm back in 1907, but the site is maintained off of an easy trail to hike while en route to paddle Boone Lake, which beings where the South Fork of the Holston River and Watauga River merge.

Take Interstate 26 west to exit 17, go north on Boone's Creek road about a mile, then left on Old Gray Station Road. After about ¾ of mile you will take a left on a gravel drive just past a 30 mph squiggly sign, then park just beyond the gray building that you will find in about ¼ mile. Cross the bridge on your left and walk up the hill to the marked site. If Boone's Creek were navigable you could paddle it down to Boone Lake where it empties, but since it is not you will need to retrace your steps and set your GPS to Interstate 26 once again, this time taking exit 13. The dam is about a mile above the TVA access just before Beulah Bridge and two small islands just before the TN 75 bridge make for a nice stop if paddling upstream.

Pioneer Paddles of the Colonial South

If you opt for downstream, the imposing peak of Bake Bluff on the south side of the river will greet you after about a mile. The riverbank is largely developed until MP 14.9 at Wahoo Valley, but if you continue you will cross under the Interstate 81 bridge into Warriors Path State Park and all of a sudden the Holston turns into Fort Patrick Henry Lake. Warriors Path was named for the Great Indian Warpath that was used by the Iroquois during raids against the Cherokee. There are two boat ramps at the marina within the park and another in the campground should you decide to begin your trek there.

Another Boone Trail area stopping point with a paddling excursion attached would be the historical marker of pioneer settler Jesse Duncan, who strayed too far from his scouting party in 1765 and was found scalped by Indians. Like his compatriot Samuel Davidson in North Carolina, Duncan is known as the first white settler to be killed by Indigenous Peoples in Tennessee. His grave lies within a family plot in Duncan's Retreat subdivision, but the marker is at the end of a dead-end road and easy to access. Take Interstate 26 to Exit 20B, stay on TN 36 north to a right on Carroll Creek Road, then it's about 2 miles to a right at the stone entry into Duncan's Retreat. After viewing the marker, follow Carroll Creek a few miles to Winged Deer Park.

Winged Deer is comprised of 200 acres on the site of a farm that operated from the 1940s to the 1970s and provides paddling access to the Watauga River's entrance into Boone Lake. Outside of the park there is a good bit of high-end development in both directions, but the numerous rock-face outcroppings remain as they appeared when Daniel first visited.

William D. Auman

A cave that locals claim goes back approximately 100 feet from the channel can be cautiously explored on the north bank of the river just upstream from the bridge. Perhaps Daniel used a poplar dugout to hide there just has he did at Boone's Cave on the Yadkin in North Carolina?

Liz prepares to enter and explore another Boone Cave on the Watauga River

Returning to the Holston, a final favorite worthy of mention would be Holston Island River Park just east of Knowville. From the launch you can paddle downstream about a mile to where it joins the French Broad and forms the headwaters of the Tennessee. You can also circumnavigate undeveloped Boyd Island for an easy out-and-back day trip with ample choices for a swim break. This park is a jewel of wilderness which is somewhat unusual in what is otherwise a

Pioneer Paddles of the Colonial South

highly populated urban area.

Last but not least, the Ocoee River Valley in southeast Tennessee is not to be missed. World class whitewater dominates this remote area of Cherokee National Forest, which was the home of the Ocoee Whitewater Center near Ducktown, venue of the 1996 Olympic canoe slalom competition, Sadly the center caught fire in 2022 and was largely destroyed. Rapids up to Class V abound and are consistently navigated by numerous outfitters and talented whitewater paddlers upstream of Parksville Lake. This author gave up his Mohawk Viper 12 rock-and-roll whitewater C-1 canoe a few decades ago, but don't let me dissuade those adventurous souls who wish to tackle the Ocoee.

For those who prefer a more moderate wilderness experience, let me suggest Kings Slough access on the western side of Parksville Lake about 4 miles off of US 74 near the town of Ocoee. From there you can launch into the heart of the national forest and view a setting that could not have changed much since the days of the Cherokee, Boone and Crockett. Greasy Creek access can be found few miles east up the road off US 74 and offers yet another opportunity for a similar experience, but your paddle upstream is limited to only about a mile as the creek becomes too shallow to navigate.

William D. Auman

Section Two: Pocahontas and Ghost Ships in the Commonwealth of Virginia

I always thought of Virginia as the "Cavalier" state, I guess in part due to the mascot of their flagship university. Yet one of the best known nicknames of the commonwealth is "Old Dominion," derived from the fact that the state was the first, and therefore the oldest, of the overseas dominions of the kings and queens of England. That makes since given the founding of Jamestown in 1607, thirteen years before the Pilgrims landed at Plymouth in Massachusetts.

On June 2, 1608, Captain John Smith and his crew set sail on the first of two voyages exploring the Chesapeake Bay region. Their first stop was the Eastern Shore near a place now known as Cape Charles. They observed indigenous members of the Accomack tribe fishing with spears from their cypress dugout canoes and were able to engage in conversation through the Algonquian language, which Smith had learned during the previous winter. The Indians directed the explorers to their village, where their chief gave them a friendly reception. According to Smith's 1624 documentary published as *"The General History of Virginia,"* he noted that the Accomack *"...spoke the language of Powhatan, wherein they made such descriptions of the bay, isles and rivers, that often did us exceeding pleasure."*

Pioneer Paddles of the Colonial South

"Indians Fishing" by John White (1540-1618) with their cypress dugouts

    The only other village included on Captain Smith's early map was Accohannock, whose chief was named Kiptopeke. Today the pioneer paddler can visit Kiptopeke State Park at Cape Charles and experience once of the most unique historical treks in the area. Fast forward to 1948, when nine World War II-era concrete ships were placed approximately ½ mile off the Cape Charles shoreline to create a breakwater for the ferry system that was employed at the time. Due to a steel shortage, these ships were built out of concrete in the early 1940s and used for transporting cargo to allied forces in Japan. Today they provide a thriving habitat for birds and marine life. It is a short paddle to circumnavigate the ships, but no one is allowed to board them. Many sandy beach areas along the northern shore can also be accessed for a private respite and swim, but be wary of the many jellyfish that have found the author's legs to be quite tasty on more than one occasion.

The Chesapeake offers numerous historical paddles that the author cannot begin to recount in an excursion chapter such as this, but do your homework online to discover many additional options to paddle in the wake of Captain Smith. I would be remiss if I failed to mention his capture by Chief Opechancanough, the brother of the paramount Powhatan Chief Wahunsenaca, together with his subsequent rescue by Wahunsenaca's daughter, Pocahontas. Legend holds that Pocahontas placed her head on top of Smith's as he was about to be clubbed by a warrior, which led to his release and adoption by Wahunsenaca, who held him in *"forever esteem as his adopted son Nantaquod."* Books and movies alike abound about the incredible life of Pocahontas, who was born in 1596 and later married English settler John Rolfe in 1614 after converting to Christianity and being baptized as "Rebecca". Many probably did not know that she had been previously married to a pirate captain known as Kocoum.

Whereas history is somewhat silent about Kocoum, the pirate we know as Blackbeard also had a connection to Virginia. Unfortunately for him, as noted in the previous chapter, such is what led to his demise at the hands of Virginian naval Lieutenant Robert Maynard. Before his death at Ocracoke Inlet he would often raid ships both off the Virginia coast and in the Chesapeake Bay. Paddlers can trek along the Atlantic or choose to access one of his favorite hiding places at First Landing State Park between Norfolk and Virginia Beach. A short paddle within Broad Bay leads to the "Narrows" along Cape Henry, where the buccaneer would drop anchor. The park is said to be near the site of the first landing on April 26, 1607 of Christopher Newport and the Virginia Company colonists who later established Jamestown.

When in the area, don't miss a visit to Jamestown where you can put yourself into the shoes of the original colonists and also paddle around three reconstructed colonial vessels in Sandy Bay near the mouth of the Back River. Further options can be found along the adjacent James Bay, which features the James Fort Archaeological Site on the coastline The original *Susan Constant, Godspeed* and *Discovery* set sail from London on December 20, 1606. As noted, the fleet reached the First Landing site in late April of 1607 before moving inland to the selected settlement site on May 13.

Other recommended explorations within the Old Dominion include the South Fork of the Shenandoah River (John Denver wrote about this gem in "Take Me Home, Country Roads," but it flows through Virginia as well as its neighbor to the west). Access areas can be found within the vicinity of the national park of the same name. The New River in the western part of the state offers everything from flat water with low-water bridge access points to a gorge filled with whitewater, similar to the James River which also features an exhilarating whitewater trail flowing through downtown Richmond.

In addition, Lake Drummond in the Great Dismal Swamp, which has an average depth of only 3 feet and is one of only two natural freshwater lakes in the Cavalier state (see section three of the previous NC chapter for historical background) has access points both at the end of Lake

William D. Auman

Drummond Wildife Drive and along the swamp's canal on Ballahack Road. Another folklore legend tells of a man whom even the devil feared, who when he died was given a red-hot coal by the devil and instructed to go to the swamp to make his own version of hell. The tortured spirit of the man can be seen at times wandering the shore of 3,142 acre lake. Moving on, as my Virginia water time pales in comparison to the other states included within this work, I encourage the reader to further explore this beautiful state and create their own supplemental entries to the excursions recommended.

Section Three: Legendary Swamps, Coastal Forts in Georgia's peachy Rivers

Perhaps the ultimate swamp'n experience of all can be found in the Okefenokee, or *"Land of the Trembling Earth,"* which covers over 700 square miles primarily in southeastern Georgia. Indigenous Peoples occupied the swamp until the early 1800s, when most were driven out or forcibly removed by European settlers. During the Second Seminole War in 1838, some fled to Fort Moniac on the St. Mary's River, while some hid in the swamp and later intermarried with early settlers. The swamp later served as a refuge for fugitives fleeing from slavery and deserters during the 1861-65 Civil War.

Whether you launch from Stephen Foster State Park on the west side, Laura S. Walker State Park on the east (both of which allow for car camping), or various spots within the refuge, *be sure to file a float plan* with the ranger or through some trustworthy individual who will come looking for you if such

Pioneer Paddles of the Colonial South

becomes necessary. This caveat is genuine and has personal roots from 1993, when the author set out from Stephen Foster in the days before smartphone GPS in an effort to reach the sill of the Suwannee River.

Some 16 miles later, with arms that later ached for a week, an exhausted author was overcome with relief when the park emerged on the horizon just after sunset. The maze of cypress that line the channels of the swamp can be confusing, but trusted maps and technology have now been developed to ensure that one can explore with the security of much greater certainty. Just don't bring Fido since you will likely see more alligators that you could ever imagine. One decided to come after a chain pickerel (known locally as a "Jack") that I had hooked while fishing, then later decided to wait for me alongside the bank while I unhooked the fish for release. I tried tossing it to the gator, who completely ignored it while continuing to stare at me. It was then that I realized that the time had come to move on.

Southeastern Georgia boasts numerous blackwater paddling and/or sea kayaking opportunities, including the Alapaha River southeast of Valdosta and the Savannah River, which defines the northern border. Another historical favorite to recommend would be a paddle along Black Island Creek to the reconstructed Fort King George near Darien. Initially built in 1721 by scouts led by Colonel John "Tuscarora Jack" Barnwell, who is buried at Saint Helena's Episcopal Churchyard in nearby Beaufort, South Carolina (see the ensuing section), the imposing sentinel represents the oldest remaining English fort on Georgia's coast. Abandoned in 1736, the site was soon occupied by Scottish Highlanders under the leadership of General James

William D. Auman

Oglethorpe.

Oglethorpe, a member of the British Parliament, had led the first shipload of 114 settlers to Savannah in 1733. Known as a man of vision, compassion and vast energy, his settlement welcomed immigrants of diverse religious views and national origins. History credits him with banning both slavery and rum from the colony that he founded. With all due respect, why would any self-respecting colonizer ban rum? Captain Jack Sparrow of *Pirates of the Caribbean* fame would likely have been tarred and feathered had he encountered General Oglethorpe!

In 1734 Oglethorpe sailed down the coast seeking strategic points to fortify and ultimately established the town of Frederica with 44 men and 72 women comprising the first settlers. They soon built a fort that served to defend British settlers from the Spanish during the War of Jenkins Ear from 1739-1748. The name of the war is derived from Robert Jenkins, a British sea captain whose ear was allegedly severed in 1731 by Spanish coast guards who were searching his ship for contraband.

By way of backdrop, Spain saw the Georgia settlements as a threat to its interests in Florida. After having repelled the English at the gates of St. Augustine, an armada of 50 vessels and 2,000 troops set sail in June of 1742 with plans to lay waste to established English communities as far north as Port Royal, South Carolina. On July 7, under Oglethorpe's command, troops from Fort Frederica and Indian allies alike routed the advancing Spanish with a fierce attack. Legend has it that the marsh ran red

Pioneer Paddles of the Colonial South

with blood from the onslaught, ending the last Spanish threat to the Georgia colony in what became known as the *Battle of Bloody Marsh*.

The remains of Fort Frederica still stand tall, yet the kayak launch at the National Monument can be difficult to navigate. One must climb the ladder attached to the lift system and use the hand crank on the dock to lower your boat into the tidal Frederica River, so be cautious! Don't forget your dolly since the launch is about a quarter mile from the visitor center.

Fort Frederica keeps vigil at St. Simon's Island

Further south we find the Crooked River, which can be accessed either at the state park which bears its name or through the Dark Entry Creek launch off of Highway 40 in St. Marys. If you opt for the former, you will find several driftwood beaches close to the access which make for a nice stopping point upon your return. If choosing the latter, take time to enjoy the salt marsh through which the creek meanders lazily alongside the Spartina, or cordgrass, before ultimately emptying into the St. Marys River. Check out the Coastal Georgia Greenway Trail and the Southeast Coast Saltwater paddling trail online for many other day trip options, including the Altamaha River.

Options for a sea-kayak day trip along the Atlantic shoreline of the southeastern Peach State abound and perhaps you will stumble upon a Spanish doubloon, reale, or piece of eight while exploring a sandy beach or tidal cave. Many other historical fort sites are waiting for time-travel exploration as well, ranging from Fort William (1738) just south of Cumberland Island to Jones Fort (1739) south of Tybee Island. Don't miss an amazing paddle to the Back River Beach area of undeveloped Little Tybee Island when putting in at the southern tip of Tybee. It is a short paddle of less than a mile across Tybee Creek to experience a coastal wilderness that has never been home to any creatures outside of native wildlife. The aspiring pioneer paddler will find a multitude of other possibilities within the region that are ripe for exploration.

Georgia has much more to offer the paddler besides its many coastal options, and as we traverse inland the terrain begins to dramatically change. The Chattahoochee National Forest near Roswell, although flowing through a primarily metropolitan suburb of Atlanta, has a designated trail system that allows one to enjoy an afternoon on the river with an easy bicycle shuttle. Although Alan Jackson sang about how much that muddy water meant to him, this stretch of the Chattahoochee River is more reminiscent of a crystal clear mountain stream.

Lake Sidney Lanier near Buford and just north of Atlanta boasts 76 recreational areas, 40 parks and campgrounds, and 10 marinas. That doesn't seem to resonate with the wilderness theme of this book, but the lake is home to hundreds of uninhabited islands that are worthy of exploration. The 38,000 acre reservoir has a tainted history in that it was formed after 1,098 Black residents of a town known as Oscarville were forcibly displaced, with the remnants of the town flooded to create the lake. The lake is said to be haunted by the spirits of those who perished in its waters and those whose graves were submerged during its creation. Ironically, the poet Sidney Lanier (who later became a lawyer) was also a Confederate private who worked on a blockade-running ship during the war.

The 323-acre Stone Mountain Lake can be found just east of Atlanta and continues to evoke a Confederate theme as well with its enormous rock relief that features carvings of Confederate President Jefferson Davis, together with Generals Robert E. Lee and Stonewall Jackson. Completed in 1972, calls are consistently heard for its removal, yet the controversy continues due to costs and firmly-held opinions on both sides of the equation. The mountain summit above the lake has an elevation of 1,686 feet, but seems much higher given that the surrounding area is quite flat. Europeans first learned of the mountain in 1567, when Spanish explorers were told by Native Americans of a mountain far inland that was "very high, shining when the sun set like a fire." Irrespective of where one falls on the political spectrum, there is a launch near the dam where you can begin to enjoy a neo-wilderness experience in the ancestral land of the Creek, not often found in urban areas.

Continuing northwest we find Tallulah Lake which offers a tranquil flat-water paddle in close proximity to a rugged gorge of the same name, which features a canyon nearly two miles long and 1,000 feet deep. Nestled nearby in remote Rabun County we have the Chattooga River, a tributary of the Tugaloo River and one of the south's premier whitewater destinations. If you haven't seen the 1972 movie *"Deliverance,"* filmed on location along section IV of the river, be sure to watch before you launch your vessel.

For a more "mild and scenic" versus "wild and scenic" section of river, the author would suggest the upper sections II or III, both laden with scenic beauty and swimming holes that are perfect for a hot summer day. These lie in the vicinity of Chattooga Town, one of the Cherokee lower towns that appeared in the 1721 British census as "Chattoogie" with only 90 inhabitants. Archaeologists believe the town was largely abandoned by 1740, but records show that the last Cherokee to live in the area, Walter Adair, sold his land in 1816.

This area is but a hop, skip and jump from the Palmetto State of South Carolina, but no Palmetto trees (also known as the Sabal or Cabbage Palm) are to be found in this remote mountain wilderness. What lies across the border, however, is worthy of a concluding excursion section within this chapter.

Pioneer Paddles of the Colonial South

Section Four: From Upstate South Carolina to a Swamp Fox in the Low Country

Perhaps the most ancient testament to life in the pre-colonial paddling south would be the Chauga Mound, whose adjacent village dates back to 8,000 B.C. Unfortunately, one must be content to paddle above where the mound now sits, as it was inundated with water back in 1962 when the Lake Hartwell Dam was completed and the reservoir began to fill. The mound now sits at the bottom of the Tugaloo River in Oconee County about 1200 feet north of the river's confluence with the Chauga River. Archaeologists were able to study the site for a few years prior to the flooding and have determined that the mound, which contained over 60 graves, was built in the 12th century and utilized last by the Cherokee as recently as early in the 18th century.

In 1540, when Hernando de Soto began his trek across "Carolina", which was not split into separate colonies until 1712, the Cherokee inhabited the northwestern corner of what is now South Carolina. Now known as the upstate region, the tribe lived in what were known as their "lower towns" which also encompassed northwest Georgia. By the middle of the seventeenth century, these towns included Jocassee, Keowee, Seneca and Toxaway. The former two sites now have namesake lakes that offer excellent flatwater paddling opportunities with spring-fed clear waters to explore. Devils Fork State Park on Lake Jocassee, encompassed by the backdrop of the rugged Jocassee Gorges, has abundant surrounding wilderness and features several waterfalls along the shoreline. Nestled alongside the calm waters of Lake Keowee we find Keowee-Toxaway State Park, home to rock outcroppings with picturesque background views of the distant Blue Ridge Mountains. In Seneca, both High Falls County Park and South Cove County Park provide additional access opportunities where one can envision paddling alongside the poplar dugouts of the Cherokee.

Many of the Cherokee clans sided with the British in the Revolutionary War, which began a dark chapter in the history of the tribe. In 1776, a multi-colony army was assembled to attack Cherokee towns with a bounty for Cherokee scalps having been authorized by the government of South Carolina. One upstate village suffered the destruction of six thousand bushels of corn, not to mention hundreds of lives lost. In 1777, the Cherokee ceded most of their land in the upstate and subsequently acknowledged the United States by signing the Treaty of Hopewell in 1785 near present-day Seneca. On March 22, 1816, they ceded their last strip of land within South Carolina. The Cherokee had resided in their lower towns for millennia, yet it took European settlers little more than 100 years to eradicate them.

Before leaving the upstate, paddlers should consider a trek along Lake Oolenoy within Table Rock State Park in Pickens County. Some of the highest mountains in the state are found within this region that was known as *Sahkanaga ("the Great Blue Hills of God")*, prior to the Hopewell treaty. In addition, Lake Bowen in Spartanburg County, although somewhat dominated by private development, has access at Anchor Park and is in close proximity to Cowpens National

Pioneer Paddles of the Colonial South

Battlefield. A pasturing area at the time of the Revolutionary War battle, the site commemorates the place where Daniel Morgan and his army turned the flanks of Banastre Tarleton's British Army on January 19, 1781.

From the upstate we traverse through the midlands and find the jewel that is known as the low country. En route, take time for the novel wilderness experience that Anne Springs Close Greenway has to offer near Fort Mill. Nestled within the ancestral home of the Catawba, this 2100 acre preserve sits on land donated by its namesake in an effort to protect remaining forest against the urban sprawl of Charlotte just to the north. Lakes Crandall, Frances and Haigler (in honor of the chief of the Catawba Nation from 1754-1763) are small, but navigable for the paddler. Although not qualifying as colonial history, Anne Close has the distinction of being the last living person to fly across the Atlantic Ocean aboard the German airship *Hindenburg* prior to its explosion in 1937.

Urban sprawl has had further impact around the capital city of Columbia, but just to the east the paddler can experience a wilderness much the same as it was for hundreds of years before—that being the Congaree Swamp. Cedar Creek is a blackwater stream that runs through the heart of the park, passing through a primeval old-growth forest with tall bluffs and an expansive floodplain that hosts an abundance of wildlife from river otters to alligators. There is a fifteen-mile marked trail that begins at Bannister's Bridge and ends at the Congaree River, but it is easy to plan for a shorter trek of six miles to Cedar Creek Landing or an out-an-back trip.

William D. Auman

Archaeological evidence suggests that humans have inhabited this area for at least 10,000 years. The Congaree tribe met Hernando de Soto of Spain in April of 1541, which brought on the eventual devastation of European disease. John Lawson commented in 1701 that *"The Congarees are kind and affable to the English...Although their Tribes and Nations border one upon the other, yet you may discern as great an Alteration in their Features and Dispositions, as you can in their Speech, which generally, proves quite different from each other, though their Nations are not above 10 or 20 miles in Distance."* History offers little after Lawson's visit, but remaining Congarees were likely absorbed by other tribes as settlers continued to encroach upon their homeland.

Not far away we find Eutaw Creek, part of the designated Swamp Fox Canoe and Camping Trail from Lake Marion to Lake Moultrie. At Catfish Landing in Eutawville, it is a short one-mile paddle to the Eutaw Springs Battlefield site next to present-day Bells Marina. The Revolutionary War battle occurred on September 8, 1781, and is considered to be the last major engagement of the war in the Carolinas. While they technically "won" the battle, the British were struck so hard by American forces under command of General Nathaniel Greene that they retreated back to Charleston and stayed there until evacuating the following year.

Fortunately for both the author and the reader, an expanse of Revolutionary War-related paddles can be found through checking out the Revolutionary Rivers National Recreation Trail online, which follows 66 miles of blackwater tributary with various access points suitable for any level of time-traveling adventure. When paddling the Lynches River from Venter's Landing it is easy to see how the war hero General Francis Marion earned his nickname "Swamp Fox." Despite being dramatically outnumbered by the British, Marion and his raiders would sneak up on the enemy, strike and then vanish into the adjoining swamp. General Marion actually took command of his militia at Venter's Landing and had a secret base camp on Snow's Island at the confluence of the Lynches and Great Pee Dee Rivers.

Before the Patriots the low-country had the Yemassee *(aka "Yamasee")*, who had migrated to low-country South Carolina from Florida in the late 16th century. In 1715 a census conducted by Irish colonist John Barnwell counted 1,220 tribal members living in 10 villages near Port Royal. Over time, some tribal members were captured by the Spanish and sold into slavery, yet ironically the Yemassee also captured members of Spanish-friendly tribes and sold them into slavery as well. Eventually the Yemassee grew tired of colonial abuse, which included a growing indebtedness due to unfair trade practices. On April 15, 1715 they decided to attack the colonial settlement of Charles Town. Large scale raids on frontier settlements continued until their defeat in 1717, which led to remaining tribal members being absorbed by the Creek and Seminole.

Although St. Augustine, Florida is generally thought of as being the oldest settlement in America, Port Royal was explored by Frenchman Jean Ribault in 1562 and predated St. Augustine by three years and Jamestown, Virginia, by 45 years. You can access the Beaufort River at Sands Beach in Port Royal and paddle upstream a short way to see the remains of Fort

William D. Auman

Frederick, the oldest surviving tabby-wall fort in the state. Built by the British between 1733 and 1755, it's most important contribution to history came over 100 years later on January 1, 1863, when people walked across a dock over the top of the fort to hear the first reading of the Emancipation Proclamation in the south. While in the area, stop by St. Helena's Anglican Church in Beaufort to see the grave of John Barnwell *("aka Tuscaroa Jack" due to having led an army against the Tuscarora of NC in 1711-1712)* who was appointed as a privateer by the English Queen Anne in 1710.

A can't miss paddle in this section of the low-country can be found on Hunting Island, a 5,000 acre semitropical barrier island 15 miles east of Beaufort. One of the few remaining undeveloped barrier islands, it offers a state park with a lagoon where one would expect to encounter Gilligan just around the bend. Paddle about a mile and a half to a where it empties into the Atlantic and you can pick a perfect spot to beach your watercraft and swim or fish before returning along the secluded waterway.

While working our way north, plan to put in at Cuckold's Creek near the town of Yemassee for an easy float towards its confluence with the Combahee River about six miles downstream. Although roughly an hour from the coast, do payattention to the tide, especially if planning an out-and-bank excursion. This serene area of roughly 350,000 acres of woods

Pioneer Paddles of the Colonial South

Those who remember Gilligan's Island would love the Hunting Island Lagoon

and wetlands passes through rice fields that were part of the former Combahee Plantation. The Combahee continues on to Beaufort and is famous for Harriet Tubman having led an expedition of 150 African American soldiers to rescue 750 former slaves in June of 1863. Hundreds of slaves boarded small boats from where they stood along the rice fields and were ultimately freed after being transported to a resettlement camp on St. Helena Island.

William D. Auman

The Edisto River, one of the longest free-flowing blackwater rivers in North America, can be found next along our trek north and has it's own canoe trail map that can be accessed online. A favorite trip from the 90s began at Colleton State Park near Walterboro and ended 23 miles later at Givens Ferry State Park, featuring an overnight camp in a secluded spot adjacent to an area farm. The current is generally mild and allows for upstream paddling should that be preferable. The Edisto ultimately enters the Atlantic near Edisto Beach State Park, which allows for paddling access to Big Bay Creek and Scott's Creek. A Native American shell midden dating back to 2000 B.C. can be found along the shoreline of the former in close proximity to the launch.

The black flag was also raised near the mouth of the Edisto going back to September of 1718, when pirate captains Charles Yeats and Charles Vane were anchored off of Sullivan's Island to the north, capturing ships as they left Charles Town harbor. After a number of disagreements, Yeats fled from Vane and sailed up the Edisto for shelter. Vane withdrew his pursuit and Yeats ultimately surrendered to be granted his Majesty's pardon. Vane, however, met his demise at the end of a rope in Port Royal, Jamaica, in March of 1721.

Pioneer Paddles of the Colonial South

Historic Fort Dorchester emerges along the banks of the Ashley River

Historic Charleston lies less than an hour north from Edisto Island and features a can't miss paddle along the Ashley River Blue Trail, one of the area's best-kept secrets for paddling and wildlife observation. The Howard Bridgman access at Bacons Bridge is a great spot to launch for a roughly 3 mile paddle past Fort Dorchester to Jessen Landing. From 1697 until the beginning of the Revolutionary War, the trading town of Dorchester flourished a mere 15 miles upriver from present-day Charleston. Only the tabby-wall fort, (constructed using a mixture of sand, oyster shells, lime ash and water), St. George's

William D. Auman

Anglican Church bell tower, and the remains of an 18th-century wharf can be seen today with forest having reclaimed the surrounding area. The fort, which arises seemingly out of nowhere as you come around a bend in the river, was built between 1757 and 1760 due to fear of a possible French invasion that never materialized.

Heading seaward, Palmetto Islands Park offers an easy launch into Horlbeck Creek, an area that still has some degree of open woodlands along the shoreline although you can't fully escape residential impacts. The imposing Wando River with its commercial traffic can be found at the mouth of the creek, but the paddler can easily venture downstream from the launch to access both scenic Tidal Creek and Boone Hall Creek. The latter takes its name from the nearby plantation which was founded in 1681 by Englishman Major John Boone.

Further downstream we find historic Sullivan's Island, point of entry for approximately 40 to 50 percent of the 400,000 enslaved Africans that were kidnapped and brought to Colonial America. During the Revolutionary War, the island was the site of a major battle at Fort Sullivan on June 28, 1776, which has since been renamed Fort Moultrie in honor of the American commander at the battle. You can paddle past the fort in the Atlantic Ocean on a calm day, but take time to disembark and pay your respects to another commander, Osceola of the Seminoles, whose grave is marked on the site and guarded by a metal fence. Osceola, who was born Billy Powell in a Creek village near the Tallapoosa River in what is now eastern Alabama, was among many Creeks who retreated to Florida after the Creek War of 1813-1814. He subsequently became a symbol of resistance and a key leader in the Second Seminole War, but was deceptively captured in 1837 while meeting General Thomas Jesup under a purported "flag of truce" to discuss peace. He died soon thereafter while imprisoned at the fort.

At the western terminus of Station 26 (streets are referred to as "stations") on Sullivan's Island you will an easy launch for an out-and-back paddle among the salt marsh of Sullivan's Narrows in the vicinity of Edgar Allen Poe's pirate treasure. While in the military Poe was stationed on the island and wrote his famous short story, *The Gold Bug,* in 1843. The story tells of a secret message hidden within parchment used to wrap a golden beetle that leads to a skull-marked tree and the buried treasure of Captain Kidd. Hopefully some day someone will actually solve the mystery Kidd's treasure since it is supposedly buried in several different states! As the reader may recall, I was unsuccessful when digging for said treasure with a plastic spoon on Money Island along the North Carolina coast.

A can't miss final spot to launch can be found at Breach Inlet between Sullivan's Island and the Isle of Palms. The inlet is much more narrow today than it was back in June 28, 1776, when hundreds of British soldiers in 15 armed flatboats attempted to cross the inlet, yet were repelled by Patriot Colonel William "Danger" Thompson and the 780 men under his command. The Americans, who had dug trenches and erected two palmetto log fortifications to protect the northern end of the island, withstood not only the invading flatboats, but also a dramatic, day-long battle against the British Navy which was supported by infantry and artillery. Imagine the sounds of cannon fire while you paddle inland along Inlet Creek and

William D. Auman

Swinton Creek while exploring Little Goat Island and other numerous undeveloped barrier islands in your search for musket balls.

Continuing north we find Francis Marion National Forest and picturesque Awendaw Creek. An easy launch lies just east of US 17 and gives paddlers the option of traveling inland towards cypress/tupelo swampland or oceanward through saltmarsh and oyster banks. Views of bluffs covered with live oak trees soon give way to open water that provides access to the Cape Romain National Wildlife Refuge and its rich mosaic of barrier islands. The Sewee Shell Mound Interpretive Trail in Awendaw is worthy of a stop as well and will lead you to a 4,000 year-old shell ring and an 800 year-old clamshell mound. These middens are the northernmost in a long chain of shell rings from Florida to South Carolina.

Another put-in (or take-out after 7 miles) option can be found at the Buck Hall Recreation area in McClellanville, but do pay attention to the tidal flow. Oyster beds are prolific so be careful not to scrape the hull of your plastic kayak across one or you may soon be sitting in a cockpit filled with water that would require a frantic retreat to shore (as beset the author back in the day!).

The Cape Romain NWR comprises 66,287 acres of coastal wilderness and extends 22 miles along the shoreline. It is home to a wild breeding program for the critically endangered

Pioneer Paddles of the Colonial South

Awendaw Creek with its enduring expanse of coastal wilderness

red wolf, a species that once spread across the entire southeastern United States. In 1980 they were declared extinct in the wild with only 14 deemed to be remaining. Those were brought into a captive breeding program and their population has now risen to over 280 in various managed care centers across the country (including the WNC Nature Center in Asheville, NC, among others), an environmental success story! You can observe them at the Sewee Visitor and Environmental Education Center before putting your boat in at Garris Landing which lies at the south of SC Road 1170.

Garris Landing, formerly known as Moore's Landing, can be found about 20 miles north of Charleston and is the only part of the Cape Romain NWR that lies on the mainland. You can take the ferry from there to Bulls Island if you feel lazy, but sea kayaking adventures abound with many small islands to be explored along the way. Archaeologists believe that the remains of the gun boat *"Planter"*, the sidewheel steamer that enslaved pilot Robert Smalls commandeered and sailed out of Charleston harbor in 1862, are buried in 12 feet of sand just off the shallow shoals that mark this area of maritime wilderness. Smalls, who would later become the first black Captain of a U.S. Navy Vessel and a U.S. Congressman, had stolen the transport and turned it over to the Union Naval Blockade early in the Civil War.

Our continuing trek northward leads to the Waccamaw River Heritage Preserve, a 30-mile strech of protected wetlands that follows the Waccamaw River in northeastern Horry County. Encompassing 5,347 acres, time seems to stand still in this region which evokes the spirit of yesterday. The Waccamaw were a tribe of Siouan origin who first appeared in historical records back in 1521. Spanish explorer Captain Francisco Gordillo named the province *Guacaya,* which in Spanish translates to Waccamaw. Fast forward to 1712, where the Waccamaw tribe joined Colonel James Moore's expedition against the Tuscarora. Ironically, in 1749 the tribe found themselves at war with the state of South Carolina and many fled to the Green Swamp in North Carolina where remaining members can be found today.

A favorite site within the preserve to launch would be Chris Anderson Landing, also known as the Highway 9 landing, in Long, South Carolina. Refer to the Waccamaw River Blue Trail map so as to tailor your trek for either a downstream float or an out-and-back adventure. Many access points along the 140 mile trial, which begins just south of North Carolina's lake of the same name, provide for a paddle steeped in history alongside what were once tribal settlements and later rice and indigo plantations. Once you reach the city of Conway, however, the neon lights of the Grand Strand begin to beckon in the distance.

Families have for generations flocked to the Grand Strand, an arc of beach land on the Atlantic Ocean that extends more than 60 miles from Little River to Winyah Bay. The focal point may be the major tourist attraction known as Myrtle Beach with its bars and roller coasters, but the pioneer paddler can escape the crowd and turn back the time machine quite conveniently with a little planning. One such spot about a half-hour inland off of US Hwy 501 would be the Little Pee Dee River, where you can put-in just upstream from Galivant's Ferry, which was one of the region's most important ferry-crossings dating back to the late 18th Century. Tidal influence is minimal here, thereby making for an easy out-and-back trip with numerous sand bars that offer a spot for a cooling swim. Do keep watch for the resident gator or perhaps the ghost of the notorious pirate Anne Bonny.

Anne and her crew had been captured back in the fall of 1720 in Negril on the west-side of Jamaica and her trial began soon thereafter on November 28. She, together with her female compatriot Mary Read and other crewmates, were found guilty of "Piracies, Felonies and Robberies committed by them on the High Sea" and sentenced to be hung. All but Anne and Mary were later hanged at Gallows Point as they were both "quick with child" and spared. Mary is believed to have died some months later, but the paper trail of Anne was not as easily documented.

William D. Auman

In 1735, Anne's father purportedly received a grant of 50 acres along the Pee Dee River, and, together with other historical findings including letters and a family bible, lends support to a local legend that he may have bribed her way out of Jamaica and aided in her disappearance. This theory was recently espoused in an episode of *Expedition Unknown's* fifteenth season. If Josh Gates became convinced that pirate treasure can be found inland along the Little Pee Dee in a low-country swamp setting, who am I to question?

A final salute to paddling the Palmetto state can begin on Williams Creek at the northernmost stretch of the Grand Strand, which features an easy launch at its Cherry Grove Beach access point. Check the tide table and paddle north towards Hog Island near the North Carolina border. You will pass the protected gem known as Heritage Shores Nature Preserve en route to Cherry Grove Point, which provides a nice respite from the overly developed shoreline that typifies the region.

CHAPTER FOUR

Safe Passages Through the Portal of Time

Whether you embark with one of your Princess Granddaughters sitting on your lap in the cockpit, or any other time and configuration when on the water, it helps to be mindful not only of wind, tide, time and distance, but also various common-sense safety precautions. That includes a float plan, emergency supplies and safety gear. You may feel that a float plan is unnecessary, but at a minimum it will serve to give your concerned family and friends peace of mind. They may still worry about the alligators or black bears that you may see, but they will know to come looking if you are not back when scheduled. Simply leave a note or send a text that includes your agenda and time of return.

Some say never to paddle alone, but there is nothing like a subjective "Zen in the moment" experience that is unique to the individual paddler. Although probably good advice from a safety standpoint, I would temper that suggestion with the same application of common sense to be utilized during a voyage of any number. Remember that caution and prevention are critical themes, and any judgment calls should be made with a healthy sense of conservatism.

As renowned canoeist Bill Riviere once commented, "paddling will never be as safe as going to prayer meeting." People do lose their lives every year, but I've never known a canoe or kayak to flip on its own accord. There will always be those who attempt to tackle rapids that are beyond their capabilities, or those who fail to take adequate precautions during the seemingly routine excursion.

Common sense, caution, and practicality account for 99% of safe passage, but it doesn't hurt to be aware of a few rules of thumb. First, make certain that at least one adult in your entourage is a competent swimmer, and ensure that ALL parties wear an appropriate personal flotation device at all times when on the water. Second, be aware of river hazards and avoid them, i.e. high water, strainers (downed trees with limbs protruding from shore), and cold. When the water and air temperatures are less than a combined 100 degrees Fahrenheit, a wetsuit or drysuit should be worn. Finally, beware of weirs and souse holes where the river drops over an obstacle, then curls back into a stationary wave. When this occurs, surface water is actually going upstream and trapping any object caught between the drop and the wave. Once trapped, a swimmer's only hope is to dive below the surface or try to swim out from the end of the wave.

You should always be aware of the difficulty classification that could be encountered during your journey. This book is devoted to the family "wilderness" experience, and therefore generally focuses on no higher than Class I or II whitewater together with many flatwater options. A few sections may include some Class III segments, which feature rapids with high, irregular waves that are capable of swamping a canoe, together with narrow passages that may require scouting, so research accordingly. In case of capsize, try to hold on to your boat and get to the upstream end so that you will not be pinned against upcoming obstacles. Keep your feet near the surface and pointed downstream, and make sure you get to slow or very shallow water before attempting to stand.

A "survival kit" is always a good idea, even for an hour-long adventure. Invest in a small dry-bag, or make your own out of a heavy duty trash bag or tackle box. Your computer-chipped car keys and smartphone will thank you for avoiding their premature demise in the event of an untimely capsize, as will your pocketbook. Emergency supplies can be anything from extra water for staying hydrated to a full-blown waterproof emergency kit depending on variables unique to your trek. Consider including matches, a whistle, knife, mirror, compass, small flashlight, space blanket, poncho, sun screen, insect repellent, candle, and a couple of energy or candy bars. If on a coastal paddle, be sure not to forget the pint of rum that will help to get you through the ordeal as was the case for Captain Jack Sparrow.

If treasure hunting, don't forget a shovel for digging so that you won't have to search for Captain Kidd's treasure with nothing more than a plastic spoon, like my friend Kyle and I were forced to do. A whistle is also a good idea and required in Florida, as are Coast Guard-approved personal flotation devices in virtually all states. Finally, consider taking along some rope so that you can tie off your watercraft and perhaps a paddle leash which is easy to attach to your cockpit. "Nuff said. Do your homework and it will be easy to make informed decisions about appropriate supplemental gear.

Last but not least, the children! Needless to say, it caused quite a stir among many when it became known that our son hit the water at age three *(see the upcoming story),* not to mention the even greater shock of our daughter starting at two. Our granddaughter Nyomi also started at three and I predict that our younger princesses, Natasha and Autumn, will likely follow suit. On another occasion from days gone by, I fondly remember my Aunt's incredulous look when I answered "yes, I have taken our kids canoeing within a stone's throw of alligators." Was I a bad parent? Well, none of us are perfect, but I think if you ask either of our young adults if paddling while toddling was a negative, a resounding "Not at all" would be their response.

Dylan and Mariah off to treasure hunt, circa 1995

      I'd like to think that we exposed them to a world of discovery and love of nature, together with their history-buff father's penchant for colonial era engagement. Any age is a good age to begin, and it's not difficult to plan an excursion that will serve as a basis for lifetime memories. A twelve year-old may not enjoy a dinosaur hunt, but perhaps a scavenger hunt for arrowheads would entice their interest on that mountain sandbar. If at the coast, there's always pirate treasure, shark teeth, shells and sand dollars to look for.

Your budding ecologist might wish to keep a checklist on the number of birds, ducks, geese, raptors, or sunbathing 'gators that you encounter. There will likely be deer, raccoon, or other animal tracks to investigate along the shoreline. Your little leaguer will enjoy the challenge of target practice using river rocks that can also be skipped along the service. If it's warm, there is nothing like a recurring swim through gentle rapids or a paddle-splashing contest.

These are but a few ideas among many. The beauty of the family experience is that you make it your own. Treasured memories are ready and waiting for you to create. Don't let any peculiar fears stand in the way of that. As noted by the late Pierre Pulling, aboriginal paddlers adhered to a fundamental safety code. First, they used good judgment. Before they acquired this judgment they depended upon someone else who had it. Second, they rarely allowed themselves to get into a dangerous situation. If, in spite of precautions, a dangerous situation was encountered, they generally had developed the skill to paddle out of it. Those time-honored standards continue to serve the contemporary paddler, so get out there and hit the water.

Returning to the "younglings," it would be remiss of me if I failed to conclude with the following article, which was originally written back in 1992 and first published by what was then known as the *Greenline* magazine, now *Mountain Express,* based in Asheville, North Carolina. It was later republished in my first book, *"Pioneer Paddling Colonial Carolina,"* which is no longer in print. I hope you enjoy reading it as much as I did writing it, and living it.

Searching for Dinosaurs by Canoe

"Daddy, look—it's a flying dinosaur!" I almost dropped our Old Town Pathfinder while removing it from the car rack, trying to see just what creature my three-year old son Dylan was referring to. In the nick of time, I caught a fleeting glimpse of two Canada geese making their way across the cove on the southern tip of Lake Keowee in upstate South Carolina. Before I had a chance to explain to my son that, no, they were not pterodactyls, additional members of the flock decided to join us on the banks of the peninsula where we intended to camp.

Dylan immediately dropped the stick he was using as his "Peter Pan sword" in defense of the squirrels at the campground, and ran to get a closer look. The first honk made him hesitate, but soon a goose was eating bread right out of his hand. Who said a February canoe-camping trip with a pre-schooler was a bad idea?

This was our first overnighter as a twosome. Needless to say, it would be a test for both of us. But this was our time to watch the ripples of wind on the water, to look for arrowheads, throw rocks, and, of course, to venture forth by boat in search of dinosaurs and other wildlife. Accordingly, the three of us (we couldn't forget Captain Planet) launched the canoe and left behind the sated geese, who seemed content to watch our journey from shore.

We couldn't have picked a better time. No offense to the Minnesota loyalists of the Boundary Waters Canoe Area, but Western North Carolinians have our own boundary waters to explore. Lake Keowee is the larger of two adjoining lakes (Jocassee is the other) in the South Carolina foothills, just off Cherokee Scenic Highway 11. To the north, the Appalachians provide a mountainous backdrop as they retreat into the Old North State. With over 225 miles of shoreline, Keowee is naturally popular with sailors and power boaters, but in two days of paddling we saw only a handful of either.

"Daddy, I want to go over there." This time it was the rocky shore of a small island filled with sweet smelling Carolina pines. Before that, it was a sandy beach near the county park where we camped. How this child maintains the stamina necessary to support his sense of adventure, I'll never know. Maybe the raccoon tracks on the soft sand, obviously made by Ninja Turtles in disguise, en route to their secret hideaway deep in the forest, had something to do with it.

We did eventually make it back to camp, and spent the remainder of the evening around the fire telling stories about the brave Indian boys (Dylan's age, of course), who used to inhabit the region. The Keowee area was once part of the Cherokee Nation, but the tribe was forced to evacuate the vicinity somewhere in the neighborhood of 1776. They subsequently lost their land after being defeated by the South Carolina militia near the end of the Revolutionary War, though many descendants of those who avoided the Trail of Tears still live on the reservation about an hour north.

When morning came, Dylan spotted a sea gull, presumably attempting a return to Myrtle Beach? A sea gull five hours from the Atlantic? In February? Surprising to say the least, but the fact that our son brought it to my attention was no longer a surprise. Thoreau once said that nature bears the close inspection of an insect's eye view, and Dylan practices that precept constantly. His eyes are level with the detail of all that is new and exciting, his imagination creating a degree of perception all its own.

Even when scattered showers came our way, the child's spirit (which by now had rubbed off on me) overcame any disappointment. The hardest thing was having to say no when Dylan wanted to pitch the tent in our backyard upon our return home. My clothes were saturated enough by then, but they'll be a next time soon.

All of you paddlers with small children can enhance your own enjoyment by including them in your journeys. Their sense of inquiry and wonder can bring a refreshing perspective to your life as a canoeist or kayaker. Once a child has conquered the fear of water and will obediently sit in a stationary position, he or she is ready for a maiden voyage. With reasonable caution and personal flotation devices, your possibilities are unlimited.

Pioneer Paddles of the Colonial South

Dylan was initiated at age 2, and now can assist with his own 30-inch paddle. Our one year-old daughter already wants to join us. Her time will soon arrive.

William D. Auman

INDEX TO REFERENCED BODIES OF WATER IN ORDER OF APPEARANCE

FLORIDA (86)

SECTION ONE: Matanzas Bay, St. John's River, Salt Run, Matanzas River and Inlet, Robinson's Creek, South Withlacoochee River, Crystal River, Homosassa River, Chassahowitzka River, Weeki Wachee River, Gulf of Mexico, Jenkins Creek, Pedersen Preserve, Airepeka Bay, Ichetucknee River, Santa Fe River, Lochloosa Lake, Rainbow River, Suwanee River, Okefenokee Swamp, Silver River

SECTION TWO: Gulf of Mexico, Pithlachascotee "Cotee" River, Crews Lake, Miller's Bayou, Werner Salt Springs, Big Bayou, Fillman's Bayou, Trouble Creek, Rocky Creek, Lake Avoca, Anclote River, Sunderland Bayou, St. Joseph's Sound, North Clearwater Harbor, Double Branch Creek, Mobbly Bayou, Upper Tampa Bay, Weedon Island Preserve, Pinellas NWR, Frenchman's Creek, Mullet Key Bayou, Hillsborough River, Green Swamp

SECTION THREE: Pine Island Sound, Big Jim Creek, J.N. "Ding" Darling NWR, Commodore Creek, Tarpon Bay, Buck Key Creek, Matlacha Pass, Buzzard Bay, Estero Bay, San Carlos Bay, Rock Creek, Orange River, Telegraph Creek, Four Mile Cove, Deerfly Creek, 4-Mile Creek, Caloosahatchee River, Lover's Key, Gulf of Mexico, Upper Manatee River, Little

Manatee River, Blackwater River, Ten Thousand Islands NWR, Kissimmeee River, Chokoloskee Bay, Halfway Creek, Barron River, Turner River, Atlantic Ocean, Indian Key Channel, Lignumvitae Key Aquatic Preserve, Long Key Lake, Curry Hammock Lagoon, Little Crawl Key Bay, Grassy Key Bay, Rachel Key Bay, Sister Creek, Boot Key Bay, Key Who Bay, Knockendown Key Bay, Big Torch Key Bay

NORTH CAROLINA (169)

SECTION ONE: Yadkin River, Roanoke Sound, Shallowbag Bay, Salmon Creek, Albemarle Sound, Chowan River, Jean Guite Creek, Pea Island NWR, Pamilco Sound, Eagle Nest Bay, North Pond, North Field Pond, South Pond, New Inlet, Atlantic Ocean

SECTION TWO: Ocracoke Inlet, Teach's Hole, Silver Lake Harbor, Beaufort Inlet, Rachel Carson Estuary, Taylor's Creek, Hoophole Creek, Town Creek (Carteret County), Core Sound, Drum Inlet, Cedar Island NWR, Pamlico Sound, Bogue Sound, White Oak River, Cow Channel, Queens Creek, Hawkins Bay, Pamlico River, Bath Creek, Goose Creek, Flatty Creek, Queen Anne's Creek, Pembroke Creek, Perquimans River, Albemarle Sound, Mill Creek, Goodwin Creek, Sutton Creek, Greenville Sound, Bradley Creek, Intracoastal Waterway, Cape Fear River, Topsail Inlet, Alligator Bay, Goose Bay, New River, Snead's Creek, Masonboro Inlet, Lockwood Folly River,

William D. Auman

Zeke's Island National Estaurine Preserve, Snow's Cut, Myrtle Grove Sound, Town Creek (Brunswick County)

SECTION THREE: Moore's Creek, Black River, Northeast Cape Fear River, Holly Shelter Creek, Ashes Creek, Lyon's Creek, Three Sisters Swamp, Merchants Millpond, Lassiter Swamp, Bennett's Creek, Contentnea Creek, Neuse River, Fort Run, Great Alamance Creek, Haw River, Trent River, Mill Creek, Bogue Sound, Catfish Lake, Great Lake, Long Lake, Little Lake, Ellis Lake, White Oak River, Cahooque Creek, Brice Creek, Lake Waccamaw, Waccamaw River, Lake Phelps, Albemarle Sound, Pamlico River, Scuppernong River, Riders Creek, Lake Mattamuskeet, Alligator River NWR, Pocosin Lakes NWR, Milltail Creek, Sawyer Lake, Rhodes Pond, Mingo Swamp, Holt's Lake, Quaker Neck Lake, Jones Lake, Salters Lake, Lake Singletary, Great Dismal Swamp, Lake Drummond, Indiantown Creek, North River, Roanoke River, Cape Fear River, Falls Lake, Pamlico Sound, Deep Riverside

SECTION FOUR: Yadkin River, Lickon Creek, Dutchman's Creek, High Rock Lake, Bear Creek, Badin Lake, Uwharrie River, Pee Dee River, Lake Tillery, Little River, Atlantic Ocean, Dan River, Kerr Scott Lake, Beaver Creek, New River, South Fork New River, North Fork New River, Mountain Island Lake, Catawba River, Gar Creek, Johnson Creek, Cowan's Ford NWR, Long Creek, South Fork River, Lake Wylie, Broad River, Lake James, South Fork Catawba River, Upper Creek, Linville River, John's

Pioneer Paddles of the Colonial South

River, Wilson's Creek, Lake Rhodhiss

SECTION FIVE: French Broad River, Tuckaseegee River, Cedar Cliff Lake, Bear Lake, Wolf Creek Lake, Tanasee Creek Lake, Lake Glenville (Thorpe Reservoir), Nantahala Lake, Nantahala River, Lake Santeelah, Little Santeelah Creek, Calderwood Reservoir, Slickrock Creek, Fontana Lake, Cheoh Reservoir, Little Tennesee River, Mouse Branch Creek, Forney Creek, Lake Hiawasee, Valley River, Hiawasee River, Swannanoa River, Big Laurel Creek, Paint Creek

TENNESSEE (19)

Douglas Lake, Clay Creek, Pigeon River, McGowan Creek, Nolichucky River, Davy Crockett Lake, Holston River, Watauga River, Clinch River, Powell River, Cumberland River, Boone's Creek, Boone Lake, Fort Patrick Henry Lake, Carroll Creek, Tennessee River, Ocoee River, Parksville Lake, Greasy Creek

William D. Auman

VIRGINIA (12)

Chesapeake Bay, Cape Charles Bay, Atlantic Ocean, Cape Henry Narrows, Broad Bay, Sandy Bay, Back River, James Bay, South Fork Shenandoah River, New River, James River, Lake Drummond

GEORGIA (18)

Okefenokee Swamp, St. Mary's River, Suwannee River, Alapaha River, Savannah River, Black Island Creek, Frederica River, Crooked River, Dark Entry Creek, Altamaha River, Atlantic Ocean, Tybee Creek, Chattahoochee River, Lake Sidney Lanier, Stone Mountain Lake, Tallulah Lake, Chattooga River, Tugaloo River

SOUTH CAROLINA (41)

Lake Hartwell, Tugaloo River, Chauga River, Lake Jocassee, Lake Keowee, Lake Oolenoy, Lake Bowen, Lake Crandall, Lake Frances, Lake Haigler, Congaree Swamp, Cedar Creek, Congaree River, Eutaw Creek, Lake Marion, Lake Moultrie, Lynches River, Great Pee Dee River,

Pioneer Paddles of the Colonial South

Beaufort River, Hunting Island Lagoon, Atlantic Ocean, Cuckold's Creek, Combahee River, Edisto River, Big Boy Creek, Scott's Creek, Ashley River, Horlbeck Creek, Wando River, Tidal Creek, Boone Hall Creek, Sullivan's Island Narrows, Breach Inlet, Inlet Creek, Swinton Creek, Awendaw Creek, Cape Romain NWR, Waccamaw River, Little Pee Dee River, Williams Creek, Heritage Shores Nature Preserve

---

William D. Auman

A WORD OF THANKS AND ACKNOWLEDGMENT

To my wife Elizabeth, for her love and companionship along our paddling odyssey that began in 1980;

To our daughter and kindred paddling spirit, Mariah Fogg, for her technical assistance and support;

To our son Dylan, who now searches for dinosaurs with his lovely daughters;

To our princess granddaughters, Nyomi, Natasha and Autumn, from their paddling Grand Poohbah;

To my friends and fellow authors from the Tarpon Springs Authors and Writers Guild, particularly John York, for their inspiration and expertise;

To my many paddling partners through the years going back to 1973, when at age 12 my parents gifted me my first boat;

To Rasta and Trouble, our primary canine paddling sidekicks;

To the many kind-hearted souls with a shared passion that we continue to meet along the way...

Pioneer Paddles of the Colonial South

www.ingramcontent.com/pod-product-compliance
Lightning Source LLC
LaVergne TN
LVHW020418070526
838199LV00055B/3659